SOLVING THE SYNOPTIC PUZZLE

Solving the Synoptic Puzzle

INTRODUCING THE CASE
FOR THE FARRER HYPOTHESIS

Eric Eve

CASCADE *Books* • Eugene, Oregon

SOLVING THE SYNOPTIC PUZZLE
Introducing the Case for the Farrer Hypothesis

Copyright © 2021 Eric Eve. All rights reserved. Except for brief quotations in critical publications or reviews, no part of this book may be reproduced in any manner without prior written permission from the publisher. Write: Permissions, Wipf and Stock Publishers, 199 W. 8th Ave., Suite 3, Eugene, OR 97401.

Cascade Books
An Imprint of Wipf and Stock Publishers
199 W. 8th Ave., Suite 3
Eugene, OR 97401

www.wipfandstock.com

PAPERBACK ISBN: 978-1-7252-8386-2
HARDCOVER ISBN: 978-1-7252-8387-9
EBOOK ISBN: 978-1-7252-8388-6

Cataloguing-in-Publication data:

Names: Eve, Eric, author.

Title: Solving the synoptic puzzle : introducing the case for the Farrer hypothesis / Eric Eve.

Description: Eugene, OR: Cascade Books, 2021 | Includes bibliographical references.

Identifiers: ISBN 978-1-7252-8386-2 (paperback) | ISBN 978-1-7252-8387-9 (hardcover) | ISBN 978-1-7252-8388-6 (ebook)

Subjects: LCSH: Bible. Gospels—Criticism, interpretation, etc. | Synoptic problem.

Classification: BS2555.52 E94 2021 (print) | BS2555.52 (ebook)

Most of the New Testament quotations are the author's own translation. A few short New Testament extracts and all Old Testament quotations are taken from the Revised Standard Version of the Bible, copyright © 1946, 1952 and 1971 by the Division of Christian Education of the National Council of Churches of Christ in the USA. Used by permission. All rights reserved worldwide.

Contents

Preface vii

Abbreviations ix

1. The Nature of the Problem 1
2. Gospel Writing in the First Century 19
3. The Two Document Hypothesis 35
4. Luke's Knowledge of Matthew 54
5. An Orderly Account? 83
6. Conclusion 110

Appendix: Suggestions for Further Reading 115

Bibliography 123

Preface

THE PRESENT BOOK AROSE out of a conversation I had with Michael Thomson over coffee in Café Rouge in Oxford's Little Clarendon Street, where we'd finally managed to meet after we kept missing each other at the 2019 conference of the British New Testament Society the week before. Michael was aware that I was working on a substantial monograph in defense of the Farrer Hypothesis for Bloomsbury T. & T. Clark's Library of New Testament Studies Series and asked if I might consider writing a much shorter introductory guide on the same topic for Cascade Books. I was very happy to do this, and the present book is the result.

This book is thus primarily aimed at students relatively new to the study of the New Testament, although it may be of interest to a wider set of people curious about the Gospels, and may also perhaps attract the attention of some fellow scholars eager to examine and criticize (or maybe even endorse) what I'm purveying. My aim has been to strike a balance between alerting readers to potential complexities and keeping things manageably simple for beginners. I have therefore striven to keep to essentials and to avoid exploring too many subsidiary issues that might obscure the main line of the argument. A certain amount of simplification has therefore been inevitable.

As part of that simplification I have avoided the distraction of footnotes or endnotes and of references to other scholarly literature in the main text (except minimally where it has seemed unavoidable). While I believe this will be helpful for my target readership, it does have a couple of potential disadvantages: the work of other scholars risks going unrecognized and the reader is left uninformed about scholarly literature on the Synoptic Problem. To meet these concerns, I have included an appendix containing an annotated list of suggestions for further reading arranged chapter by chapter together with a bibliography (to which the appendix refers).

Preface

Since this book assumes a readership with no knowledge of Greek, I have resorted to inelegant English translations of parallel passages in an attempt to reproduce the pattern of agreements and disagreements in the underlying Greek. Where I have considered it helpful to discuss particular words or phrases in the original Greek, I have done so by giving them both in the Greek alphabet and in transliteration along with an English translation. This may help introduce a smattering of New Testament Greek to total beginners. It should also help readers who already have some knowledge of Greek, since for such readers Greek words and phrases may look clearer when presented in the Greek alphabet than when transliterated.

When we were talking in Café Rouge, Michael Thomson gave me the option between writing a general introduction to the Synoptic Problem and writing one advocating the Farrer Hypothesis. We quickly settled on the latter; it seems better to advocate openly rather than feign neutrality. While I hope this little book will prove persuasive, I also hope readers who are new to the Synoptic Problem will also read scholars who advocate other views so that they become better equipped to appreciate competing views and decide between them for themselves.

Abbreviations

2DH	Two Document Hypothesis
2GH	Two Gospel Hypothesis
BETL	Bibliotecha ephemeridum theologicarum lovaniensum
DT	Double Tradition
ETL	*Ephemerides theologicae Lovanienses*
FH	Farrer Hypothesis
GRBS	*Greek, Roman and Byzantine Studies*
ICC	International Critical Commentary
JHS	*Journal of Hellenic Studies*
JSNT	*Journal for the Study of the New Testament*
JSNTSup	Journal for the Study of the New Testament, Supplements
LNTS	Library of New Testament Studies
MPH	Matthean Posteriority Hypothesis
NTGL	The New Testament and Greek Literature
NTM	New Testament Monographs
NovT	*Novum Testamentum*
NTS	*New Testament Studies*
SAC	Studies in Antiquity & Christianity
SNTSMS	Society for New Testament Studies Monograph Series
TT	Triple Tradition

1

The Nature of the Problem

WHERE DID THE EVANGELISTS (the people who wrote the Gospels) get their material from? Much of it will have come from some overlapping combination of oral tradition, memory (both individual and collective), and the life, preaching, practice, and teaching of the first Christians. But it is also likely that at least some—and perhaps quite a lot—of what's in the Gospels derives from written sources. While many of these written sources may have been lost, some may survive within the pages of the New Testament, particularly if any of the Evangelists drew on the work of one or more of the other Evangelists whose Gospels survive.

For reasons we'll see shortly, this looks particularly likely in relation to Matthew, Mark, and Luke. The *Synoptic Problem* is the attempt to trace the literary relationship between these three Gospels. What constitutes the best solution to the Synoptic Problem continues to be contested, since none of the theories proposed is entirely without its difficulties. Since the mid-nineteenth century, the dominant solution has been the Two Document Hypothesis (the theory that Matthew and Luke made independent use of Mark and something called Q, which we'll explain below). The Two Document Hypothesis (or 2DH) has never gone wholly unchallenged, but introductory treatments to the Synoptic Problem often treat it as the obvious frontrunner, while giving short shrift to alternative views (a notable exception being Mark Goodacre's *The Synoptic Problem: A Way Through the Maze*, which favors one of the 2DH's main rivals, the Farrer Hypothesis). This short book will explore some of the main arguments that have sustained the 2DH but, like Goodacre, will argue for the Farrer Hypothesis.

But we should first begin with a broader overview of what the Synoptic Problem is about, what is at stake, and why it is has proved difficult to come to an agreed solution.

Preliminary Overview

If we compare the four canonical Gospels, we will see that John stands somewhat apart from the other three in tone, content, and structure. While Matthew, Mark, and Luke clearly differ among themselves, they just as clearly resemble one another in many significant ways, not least in the general course of events they describe, a good many specific incidents and sayings, and similarities of wording. For this reason, they are generally grouped together as the *Synoptic Gospels*, meaning that they can usefully be viewed together, especially in a *synopsis*, a book that lays out the Gospels in parallel columns.

Closer comparison of the three Synoptic Gospels reveals the following main points:

1. The material common to all three (the so-called Triple Tradition) is roughly the same as the content of Mark, the main (though not sole) exception being that Luke largely lacks parallels to the material in Mark 6:45—8:26.

2. With some notable exceptions (such as Matthew chapters 8–9) the material common to all three Synoptic Gospels largely appears in the same order in all three. Where either Matthew or Luke differs from Mark's order, the other nearly always agrees with it.

3. Matthew and Luke additionally have quite a bit of material in common (the so-called Double Tradition) that is not found in Mark.

4. Each Synoptic Gospel has material peculiar to itself, although the amount of material peculiar to Mark is very small.

5. The wording of material common to two or three Gospels can often be remarkably similar, but can also be substantially different, and this varies from one set of parallels to another.

6. There are many places where two of the Gospels agree in wording (and sometimes in other ways) against the third, and this is the case for each pair of Gospels (that is, Matthew and Mark can agree against Luke, or Luke and Mark against Matthew, or Luke and Matthew against Mark).

The Nature of the Problem

The question posed by the Synoptic Problem is how this set of similarities and differences came about. That we still talk about the Synoptic *Problem* should warn us that the question may be trickier than it looks. The six main points listed above are all set out in quite general terms, and at that level of generality all sorts of different answers can be made to appear plausible; as so often in life, the devil lurks in the detail. We shall dive into some of that detail in the chapters that follow, but before doing so we should first sketch out the different kinds of solution on offer and some of the things we might need take into account when evaluating them.

If you've never thought much about the relationship between the Gospels before, you may think that the reason Matthew, Mark, and Luke are so similar is simply because they are describing the same events, and the reason they differ in detail is simply because they do so from slightly different points of view. Of course, that's true up to a point, but it doesn't really explain the particular kinds of similarities and differences we see. Few people have ever thought that all three Synoptic Gospels were eyewitness accounts, and few scholars today believe that any of them are (although most would accept that eyewitness accounts must presumably underlie much of the material they contain). For one thing, the Gospels hardly read as bare eyewitness accounts of what took place; in one way or another they are all concerned to bring out the significance of these events for Christian faith and practice; a lot of reflection has gone into their composition. For another, the suggestion that the Gospels are more or less variant first-hand accounts of what took place fails to explain why the three Synoptic Gospels cluster together while John is so different and makes no serious attempt to address the specifics of the points listed above. In particular, it is difficult to see how three Evangelists writing independently of one another should end up agreeing, not simply on the basic facts, but in the ordering and wording of their accounts to the extent that they do.

A more sophisticated form of this initial suggestion (that has both a long pedigree and some modern defenders) proposes that Matthew, Mark, and Luke each worked from a common oral tradition. On this model, the pattern of variation and similarities between the Gospels is what might be expected from various performances of the same underlying oral tradition, rather in the way that variant accounts of the same basic story might appear in folklore or oral epic poetry. But there are rather too many difficulties with this view for it to attract the majority of modern scholars.

Perhaps the most common objection is that this oral gospel hypothesis fails to account for the extent of common wording and common order apparent in the Synoptic Gospels. While oral tradition can produce more agreement in order and wording than the intuitions of modern scholars may allow, several cogent objections remain. First, there is the difficulty of explaining how an oral tradition that presumably began in Aramaic (the language most likely spoken by Jesus and his immediate disciples) gave rise to close verbal agreements in Greek. Second, the first-century Mediterranean world was not a purely oral culture unaffected by writing. Even if a case can be made for a substantial degree of residual orality in Mark (meaning that its language often appears closer to an oral than a written register), the other Gospels look more consciously literary. Their genre resembles that of contemporary *bioi* (or lives, the ancient equivalent of biographies), and the variations between them often reflect the kinds of changes ancient writers typically made to their written sources. Again, despite differences between individual manuscripts of Matthew, Mark, and Luke, by and large these three Gospels remain three quite distinct compositions. What survives are (broadly speaking) three discrete Synoptic Gospels, not a continuous spread of written transcripts of variant oral performances.

Most scholars therefore believe that the Synoptic Problem demands a *literary* solution, an answer in terms of a relationship between written texts. This is not to deny that oral tradition may also have played an important role in the composition of the gospels, but it is to maintain that the Synoptic Problem is *primarily* about the Evangelists' use of written sources.

The question then arises what these written sources were and where to look for them. There's no guarantee that any or all of these sources survived, but one approach is to focus on those that have and to see if the similarities and differences between the Synoptic Gospels can be plausibly accounted for (or at least, largely accounted for) on the basis of a direct literary relation between them. While such *utilization* hypotheses (as they are often called) could in principle take in other surviving texts (such as the Gospel of John, or the letters of Paul, or early non-canonical texts such as the *Didache*), in practice they tend to focus primarily on the three Synoptic Gospels. Pure utilization hypotheses generally propose that the first Gospel to be written was used as a source by whichever Gospel came second, and that the third then used the other two. In principle, this allows for six possible combinations:

The Nature of the Problem

1. Matt → Mark → Luke (Augustinian Hypothesis, or AH)
2. Matt → Luke → Mark (Two Gospel Hypothesis, or 2GH)
3. Mark → Matt → Luke (Farrer Hypothesis, or FH)
4. Mark → Luke → Matt (Matthean Posteriority Hypothesis, or MPH)
5. Luke → Matt → Mark
6. Luke → Mark → Matt

In practice, few scholars support (5) or (6) (while the Jerusalem School proposes that Luke may be the earliest Gospel, it invokes lost sources in addition and so is not a pure utilization hypothesis). Of the remaining four the Augustinian Hypothesis is so called because it is attributed to St. Augustine of Hippo (although it has been questioned whether he actually held it), which would make it the earliest literary solution to the Synoptic Problem we know of. The second, the Two Gospel Hypothesis, was (in an earlier form), first proposed by Johann Jakob Griesbach in the eighteenth century, making it the earliest scholarly synoptic hypothesis of modern times (and the dominant one up until the mid-nineteenth century). It was revived in the mid-twentieth century by William Farmer and for a time became the main challenger to the dominant Two Document Hypothesis. The third (the Farrer Hypothesis) has its roots in the nineteenth century and has been gradually gaining momentum since the publication of Austin Farrer's 1955 essay "On Dispensing with Q" and its subsequent espousal by scholars such as Michael Goulder and Mark Goodacre. The fourth, the Matthean Priority Hypothesis, has been proposed (albeit rather sketchily) by a handful of scholars such as Martin Hengel and Ronald Huggins, and more recently explored in more depth in a book by Robert MacEwen; but it as yet has few other followers.

A diametrically opposed approach argues that there is no *direct* literary relationship between any of the Gospels, but that the pattern of similarities and differences they exhibit is to be explained on the basis of their now lost source or sources. An early form of this theory postulated a single ur-Gospel, a primitive written account supposedly used independently by all three extant Synoptic Gospels, but this has fallen out of favor since the nineteenth century. More recent proposals, such as those of M.-E. Boismard and Delbert Burkett, have invoked multiple hypothetical lost sources supposedly used in various combinations by Matthew, Mark, and Luke.

Such proposals are not simply the result of perverse refusals to accept simpler solutions; they are motivated by genuinely perceived difficulties in direct utilization hypotheses, not least the belief that there is no clear direction of dependence between any pair of the Synoptic Gospels. Proponents of such multiple source hypotheses argue that simpler theories are unworkable because they fail to do justice to the data. For example, while there may be many good reasons for supposing that Matthew used Mark, they are (it is argued) undermined by other indications that Mark must have used Matthew or that Matthew was either unaware of or unaccountably avoided certain features of Mark's Gospel, such as word-choice or the ordering of certain miracle stories. Thus, it is argued, since neither Matthew nor Mark could have used the other, the similarities between them must be due to their independent use of one or more common sources (and likewise for Matthew and Luke and for Mark and Luke).

Yet, while such multiple-source theories have some value in calling attention to the complexity of the data to be explained, they are nevertheless open to criticism on several important grounds. The first is that they are effectively untestable: the greater the number of purely hypothetical lost sources that are invoked, the less confidence we can have in the proposed reconstruction of any individual lost source, so that while complex multiple-source theories may be capable of explaining the data, in a sense they do so too easily. Without knowing the precise wording and contours of any given hypothetical source, we are unable to scrutinize the way they are meant to work together in any detail. Such multiple-source theories are unlikely to prove fruitful, since by being capable of explaining anything they end up effectively explaining nothing (if we don't have much idea of what the Evangelists' sources looked like, we gain very little insight into how they used their sources).

A second criticism is that there is no independent evidence that any of the proposed hypothetical sources existed. While this objection isn't fatal—it is by no means impossible that earlier sources should have been lost because no one bothered to make any further copies of them once our extant Gospels superseded them—it invites doubt whether the multiplication of such purely hypothetical sources is really necessary.

A third criticism is whether such multiple source hypotheses involve a plausible picture of how the Evangelists are likely to have worked. On the one hand they tend to require the Gospel writers to have conflated (i.e., closely stitched together) multiple sources, while on the other they often envisage them doing so in a rather mechanical way, since they tend to attribute the differences between the Gospels rather more to the Evangelists' sources than to the Evangelists' creative editorial (or compositional) activity. Neither assumption seems plausible.

At first sight, the Two Document Hypothesis (2DH) represents an ideal compromise between pure utilization hypotheses and multiple-source hypotheses, addressing many of the supposed difficulties of the former without resorting to the Byzantine complexities of the latter. In essence, the Two Document Hypothesis (2DH) proposes that Matthew and Luke made independent use both of Mark and of a second, now lost, source scholars call Q (from the German *Quelle*, meaning "source"). This solution is commonly presented in the form of the following diagram:

FIGURE 1

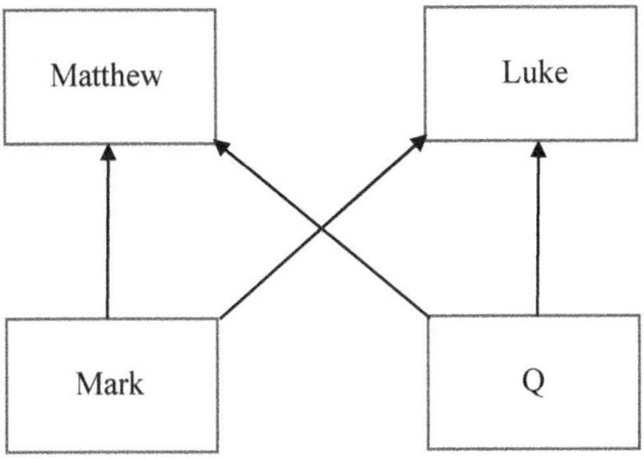

[Diagram: Matthew and Luke boxes at top, with arrows coming up from Mark and Q boxes at bottom, crossing in the middle]

The Two Document Hypothesis

On this solution, the Triple Tradition (the material common to all three Synoptic Gospels) is explained by Matthew's and Luke's use of Mark, and the Double Tradition (the material common to Matthew and Luke but not found in Mark) is explained by their use of Q, while the differences between Matthew and Luke are explained by their having independently used Mark and Q in different ways.

On the face of it this is a simple and elegant solution. It involves only one hypothetical lost source, Q, and although there is virtually no external evidence that Q ever existed (apart from one much-debated passage in the ancient author Papias, which almost certainly doesn't refer to Q), it is at least initially plausible that early Christians would have ceased to copy something like Q once its contents were fully absorbed into Matthew and Luke (and since manuscripts wear out with use, texts that cease to be copied generally fail to survive). Moreover, unlike the hypothetical sources in more complex multiple-source theories, Q is quite tightly defined. It comprises the material common to Matthew and Luke but not found in Mark (plus a few passages supposedly common to Mark and Q, a point to which we shall return later). Since Luke is generally faithful to Mark's order, his Gospel is assumed to be equally faithful to Q's order. On this assumption, together with the assumption that Matthew and Luke both incorporated the entirety of Q into their own Gospels, we can reconstruct the content, order, and even much of the wording of Q with a fair amount of apparent precision.

This reconstruction nevertheless relies on several assumptions we might want to question. Given that Mark is largely a narrative source and Q is mainly comprised of sayings, it is not obvious that Luke would necessarily treat them both in much the same way (Matthew clearly couldn't have done). Given that Matthew omits some Markan passages and Luke omits quite a few of them, it's surely unsafe to assume that both Evangelists incorporated the entirety of Q. Since the 2DH needs to postulate passages in which Mark and Q overlap (a point to which we shall return), it is unclear why the extent of Mark–Q overlaps should be restricted to just those that are apparent through Q having the fuller account (which Matthew and Luke both chose to use); there could be other cases where Mark's account is fuller (so Q's is now invisible), or where either Matthew or Luke (but not both) chose to follow a Q version of a passage where the other has followed Mark. On the basis of the evidence we have, Q could contain a great deal more material in common with Mark than we can now discern.

That said, reconstructing Q on the basis of the standard assumptions does have the merit of making the 2DH both definite enough to be held to account and precise enough to be potentially fruitful. While there are inevitable uncertainties about the precise extent and wording of Q, what can be reconstructed with reasonable confidence is a text whose outlines are clear enough to be useful. Despite the uncertainties that remain, Q is text that is definite enough for its shape, contents, and ideas to be worth discussing along with its role in the composition of Matthew and Luke. Q, as tightly defined by its responsible advocates, contributes to a hypothesis that is *testable*, since it presents a sufficiently stable target for its critics to engage.

The Nature of the Problem

For these reasons, the clear assumptions that lead to a tightly-defined Q are greatly preferable to looser notions that suggest Q might be a stream of tradition or a collection of documents or some other protean entity that can shape-shift according to need and so escape any possibility of serious criticism. A vague, amorphous Q is an entity that can adapt itself to meet any problem. A tightly defined Q is worthy of respect as an integral part of a serious hypothesis. The latter is accordingly the form of the Two Document Hypothesis with which we shall engage here.

So let us be quite clear what exactly we shall take "Q" to mean. Q is a hypothetical single document whose extent, content, and order is reconstructed on the following set of assumptions: (1) Matthew and Luke made independent use of Q along with independent use of Mark; (2) Q accounts for all the material common to Matthew and Luke not found in Mark plus some material found partly in Mark but expanded or substantially changed in similar ways by both Matthew and Luke; (3) Matthew and Luke incorporated the whole of Q into their own compositions; and (4) for the most part (with one or two possible exceptions), the order of material in Q is the same as the order of the Double Tradition material in Luke.

Calling Q hypothetical is *not* intended to condemn it for being so. Any solution to the Synoptic Problem can only be a hypothesis, and to condemn a hypothesis for being hypothetical would be absurd. But calling Q hypothetical *is* meant to draw attention to the fact that it exists only as part of a wider hypothesis (the Two Document Hypothesis). No manuscript of Q has ever been found. No ancient author refers to any text that is at all likely to have been Q. Calling Q hypothetical is *also* intended to emphasize that Q functions as part of a particular hypothesis (the 2DH). "Q" is not a catch-all term for any pre-Gospel written source whatsoever that may be invoked as part of any source-critical theory whatsoever; using "Q" to refer to other sources that don't meet the tight definition given above is as unhelpful as using the word "electron" as a generic term for all kinds of subatomic particle. Thus, for example, to suggest (as some scholars occasionally do) that Luke may have used Matthew, Mark, *and* Q, is to miss the point that if Luke used a third source alongside Matthew and Mark, that source cannot have been Q (as defined above), since the way in which the third source should be reconstructed (and hence the text that results) must inevitably differ from the way in which Q is reconstructed (the same assumptions simply cannot apply in both cases). This is not to rule out the possibility of a three-source hypothesis in which Luke used Matthew, Mark, and another source he had in common with Matthew; it is just to insist that such a hypothetical third source should be called something other than Q and the resulting hypothesis something other than the Two Document Hypothesis.

But why do we need Q at all? On the face of it, that Luke and Matthew share material not found in Mark could be the result of one of them taking it from the other (as we shall be arguing here). So why introduce a purely hypothetical source for which there is no external evidence whatsoever? Historically, some of the reasons for introducing Q may have been dubious (such as the almost certainly mistaken belief that Papias was referring to a sayings-source—the so-called Logia source—he attributed to Matthew, and the apparent desirability of unearthing an early source for Jesus' sayings). But the important arguments for Q rely principally on the alleged difficulty of envisaging the way in which Luke would have to have used Matthew (or vice versa). We shall examine these alleged difficulties in later chapters, as well as identifying similarities between Matthew and Luke that make their mutual independence look unlikely.

The Farrer Hypothesis, which we will be arguing for here, is often represented by the following diagram (which dispenses with Q):

FIGURE 2

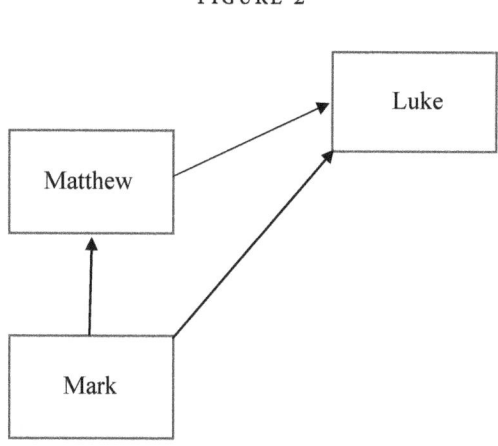

The Farrer Hypothesis

It will be seen that while the Two Document Hypothesis and the Farrer Hypothesis disagree on the need for Q, they agree that Mark came first and was at least one of the principal sources for both Matthew and

Luke. This part of the thesis is known as Markan Priority. Not everyone agrees with it, however. Some patristic testimony can be seen as suggesting that Matthew's Gospel was the earliest to be written (in part because its author was identified with Matthew the tax-collector who was a disciple of Jesus, a view not widely shared by modern scholars). And as we have seen, the thesis of Matthean Priority was also propounded by Griesbach in the eighteenth century and revived by Farmer in the twentieth. That Matthean Priority continues to attract at least some support shows that Markan Priority is not a done deal, however convincing it may seem to many scholars. Markan Priority is (we shall argue) a well-grounded hypothesis, but it is not an objective fact established beyond all reasonable doubt.

It may look as if the six main points we set out on page 2 point to Mark being earliest of the three Synoptic Gospels. That Mark is the shortest of the three and comprises virtually all the material they share seems most naturally to suggest that Matthew and Luke both expanded on Mark with additional material. That either Matthew or Luke, and very often both, largely agree with Mark's order can be taken as suggesting that Mark's order was the basis of that of the other two. Additionally, that Matthew's Greek and Luke's Greek are generally better than Mark's also seems to suggest that they each improved on Mark's Gospel. Yet while all these points have been urged in support of Markan priority, they are not (at least as stated in such broad terms) as conclusive as they were once thought to be; the six general points listed at the start of this overview are compatible with any order of composition of the Gospels. Rather more detailed arguments are needed to determine which order this is most likely to have been.

We shall return to these arguments in chapter 3, but there are a few other things we need to think about first. Over the last several decades, the debate over the plausibility or otherwise of Luke's use of Matthew (and hence the need for Q) has shifted from judgments about what Luke might have been motivated to do artistically (for example, whether or not Luke could have had any possible reason for rearranging Matthew's Double Tradition material into an allegedly inferior order) to a more fruitful examination of how far what the Evangelists would need to have done with their sources on the various different source-critical theories plausibly matches the working methods of their contemporaries. We shall sketch out some of the background to this discussion in chapter 2. But in the remainder of this chapter we'll address a couple of prior questions: what can we reasonably expect of a source-critical theory, and why should we care about the Synoptic Problem in the first place?

What Kind of Hypothesis?

We've said that Q is a hypothesis, Markan Priority is a hypothesis, and any theory of relationships between the Gospels is a hypothesis. But what exactly do we mean by a "hypothesis" in this context? What do we expect a hypothesis to achieve? Do we want it to describe what we think actually happened, or do we want it to provide a useful model of Synoptic relations that we can go on to use for other purposes? Ideally, we would no doubt want both, but what if these two aims conflict? What if what actually happened was so complex and messy that trying to reconstruct it from the surviving texts is an impossible task, and that even if we were to succeed in that impossible task the resulting account turned out to be so convoluted that we could neither grasp it nor make any use of it?

In practice, leading solutions to the Synoptic Problem tend to be those that compromise between trying to describe what actually happened and developing a model that is straightforward enough to be both testable and usable. Such a model will be the most economical account that does reasonable justice to the surviving data, while allowing (a) that the model may be incomplete (the Evangelists may well have been influenced by other factors and used other sources that the model does not account for) so that (b) some (but hopefully not too much) of the surviving data may not fit the model as comfortably as we should ideally like. You'll probably have noticed that the foregoing definition contains several terms (such as "most economical," "reasonable justice," and "hopefully not too much") that are open to subjective interpretation. In the end these are matters of informed scholarly judgment on which different people may honestly and reasonably disagree. But while disagreements at this level may well contribute to ongoing disagreements about the best solution to the Synoptic Problem, they do not undermine the possibility of meaningful debate. Most of us share sufficiently similar notions of economy and reasonableness that we can usefully argue which model of synoptic relations best provides them.

No model of synoptic relations can hope to account for absolutely everything that went into the composition of the Gospels. Only a fraction of the evidence we would need to construct a complete picture of what actually happened has survived. Before any account of Jesus' life was written

The Nature of the Problem

down, stories of his deeds and preaching would have been passed on by word of mouth. This oral tradition didn't immediately grind to a shuddering halt with the writing of the first Gospel. If Matthew and Luke both made use of Mark, that does not mean that they didn't also know some of the sayings and stories in Mark from other sources (oral and perhaps written as well), and their knowledge of those other versions may well have influenced what they wrote. But we have no way of knowing this for sure in any individual instance, since the oral tradition no longer survives for us to listen to. We might venture guesses what it contained based on the surviving written evidence, but guesses—albeit informed guesses—are as much as they can ever be. Similarly, even if Mark was the first Gospel to be written, he may well not have been the first to commit Jesus material to writing, even if only in the form of notes for preaching, or collections of Jesus' sayings or miracles for private use. Some such pre-Markan notes may have been known to Mark or to one or more of the other Evangelists, but we have no way of knowing this for sure (despite the occasional efforts of some scholars to reconstruct such sources).

We therefore need to recognize that neat diagrams of synoptic relationships won't give us the full picture. In particular, the theory that Matthew and Luke used Mark and Q (2DH), or that Matthew used Mark and that Luke used Mark and Matthew (FH), should not be taken as implying that Matthew and Luke used Mark and Q *and absolutely nothing else*, or that Matthew used Mark *and absolutely nothing else* and Luke used Mark and Matthew *and absolutely nothing else*. These hypotheses are better understood as suggesting where known texts (Matthew, Mark, and Luke) fit into the wider picture, along with one hypothetical text (in the case of the 2DH) that can be reconstructed with reasonable confidence, without at all claiming that the relationships between just this set of texts accounts for everything that went into the composition of the Gospels.

Thus any proposed solution to the Synoptic Problem of the kind we shall be discussing here is a model that aims to be a reasonable approximation to what we think most likely in fact happened without trying to account for all of it. But this leaves us with a dilemma in how we should go about arguing for and against the relative merits of competing theories. Do we argue as if the data have to be explained solely on the basis of the documents that explicitly feature in any given hypothesis (so that, for example, the FH has to account for Luke's Double Tradition solely on the basis of Luke's use of Matthew)? We might call this the "strict" approach. Or do we allow ourselves to appeal to otherwise unknown but historically plausible factors (such as an oral tradition of the Lord's Prayer) to get over what might otherwise be difficulties for our favored hypothesis? We might label this the "loose" approach. Taking the strict approach leaves us open to the charge of appearing historically implausible (isn't it likely that Luke knew the Lord's Prayer before he saw it in Matthew?). Taking the loose one leaves us open to the charge of appearing ad hoc, that is, of using ultimately unknowable factors such as oral tradition as a set of get-out-of jail-free cards to insulate our favored theory from criticism. This dilemma threatens to leave us in a "heads I win, tails you lose" situation.

The best way through this dilemma, I suggest, is to adopt the following two principles: (1) that sauce for the goose is sauce for the gander, in other words that the same (strict or loose) approach should be applied fairly and consistently in evaluating all the theories being discussed; and (2) that the strict approach should be followed as far as possible. The more we try to give a plausible explanation for how a later Evangelist made use of the earlier source or sources required by any given model in terms of that model alone, the more stringently we are testing the model, and other things being equal, it is better to risk erring on the side of excess stringency. If, for example, we can provide a plausible explanation of Luke's use of Matthew (perhaps in conjunction with Mark) in every place the 2DH explains Matthew and Luke on the basis of their use of Q (perhaps in conjunction with Mark), then we shall have provided a strong argument in favor of the FH, even though on occasion we may have been more stringent than strictly necessary. That said, the qualification "as far as possible" is a recognition both that we may be being more stringent than necessary and that there may be places where we are forced to concede that the explanation we've offered is not as neat as we'd ideally like (and where other influences may in fact have come into play). Obviously, it's best if such cases can be kept to a minimum. (Just for the avoidance of doubt, we should emphasize that even the strictest approach doesn't exclude our appealing to additional oral or written sources to explain material outside the scope of the particular hypothesis we're looking at, such as material that's peculiar to Matthew or to Luke, on both the 2DH and the FH, plus other non-Markan material in Matthew, on the FH; Michael Goulder largely excluded such sources from his version of the FH, but his view is not the norm).

The choice between loose and strict approaches also applies to how we envisage the Evangelists working. At one extreme we could take an extremely strict approach in which everything has to be explained on the assumption that the Evangelists wrote their Gospels in one go by working directly from their sources. At the other we could take a far looser approach that envisages the Gospels taking shape through a series of multiple drafts involving collaborative effort and extending to variant versions behind the texts we now have. This loose approach may well reflect historical reality rather better than the extremely strict approach (we'll say a bit more about that in the next chapter). Yet many discussions of the Synoptic Problem proceed on something more closely resembling the extremely strict approach. While this may seem justified on the same grounds as before (it's best to err on the side of subjecting hypotheses to the most stringent possible approach), it risks employing assumptions that are too remote from historical plausibility to be worthwhile. This is another issue to which we'll return in the next chapter, when we'll develop a more intermediate, qualified strict approach.

The questions of the Evangelists' sources and their working methods come together in the issue of how they may plausibly have adapted their sources. Again, this is something we'll look at more closely in the next chapter, but it's worth highlighting a couple of points right away. The first is that arguments about the direction of dependence are frequently reversible (for example, did A expand B or did B compress A?). The second is that faced with any two texts A and B and the assumption that B used A, we can always come up with some tolerably plausible explanation after the fact for why the author of B adapted A as he would have to have done. But what counts as tolerable plausibility may often be a matter of subjective judgment. The element of subjectivity can be reduced if we can show that B's supposed changes to A are in line with what B does elsewhere and/or with how other ancient authors typically adapted their sources. This is something else we shall need to consider further in the next chapter.

Why Does it Matter?

By this point you may be wondering, why does any of this matter? The Synoptic Problem may present an intriguing puzzle for people who like that sort of thing, but why should anyone else care who used what and why? Why not just enjoy the Gospels as our Bibles present them to us?

For many purposes this may suffice. The Gospels can be used in church or devotional reading or appreciated as stories without worrying too much how they came to be written. A substantial amount of worthwhile scholarship can be done on the Gospels in their final, canonical form, without entering into questions of source criticism or Synoptic relations. But quite apart from the fact that biblical scholarship also tends to venture into areas where source criticism can't be ignored, many popular claims about what the Gospels teach, or about what Jesus said and did, are hardly left untouched by the Synoptic Problem.

This is most obvious at the level of the Historical Jesus (an ambiguous term that slides between referring to what the historical person Jesus of Nazareth actually said and did and what we can most plausibly reconstruct about him by employing the current methods of critical historical research—senses that overlap without coinciding). At the most basic level, if there is some kind of literary relationship between the three Synoptic Gospels, it simply won't do to treat them as if they were independent witnesses to what Jesus said and did. For example, if Matthew and Luke derived much of their narrative from Mark, the fact that all three Gospels contain similar stories of Jesus healing a paralytic or telling the parable of the sower does not mean that we have three independent accounts of these events or that that they are triply attested. One may perhaps make the case that Matthew's and Luke's willingness to take these accounts over from Mark implies that they regarded them as at least plausible, which may lend indirect support to Mark, but that is an argument of a rather different kind.

On the other hand, if the 2DH is correct and there once was a documentary Q that was independent of Mark, then Q would potentially be an independent witness to at least some events in the life of Jesus (such as his Temptation) and even more so to many of the things that Jesus is supposed to have taught. Independent witness does not amount to historical proof, but it nevertheless figures in discussions of the Historical Jesus. Conversely, if Q never existed (as on the FH, 2GH, MPH and AH), then it cannot be appealed to as an independent witness to the Jesus tradition.

The Synoptic Problem also impacts our understanding of the early development of the Jesus tradition. Most obviously, different solutions entail different (relative) datings for the composition of the various Gospels. For example, any theory involving Markan priority necessarily implies that Mark was written before Matthew and Luke. The 2DH would seem to imply that Matthew and Luke were written around the same time as each other, otherwise it becomes increasingly difficult to envisage the earlier of these two Gospels being unknown to the author of the later one. On the other

The Nature of the Problem

hand, the FH implies not only that Luke must have been written after Matthew (as well as after Mark), but also long enough after Matthew for Luke to have taken account of it.

Some (though by no means all) advocates of Q have gone on to discuss its theology, its stages of composition, and the social history of the community that used it. Because Q has very little narrative and no passion narrative (account of the arrest, trial, death and resurrection of Jesus), studies of this sort sometimes end up proposing the existence of a variety of primitive Christianity for which the death and resurrection of Jesus were not all that important and Jesus was remembered primarily as a teacher of wisdom, perhaps a little like some of the Cynic sages, with Jesus' more apocalyptic teaching (his pronouncements on topics like judgment and the second coming) being added to a later version of Q in light of the Q community's experience of rejection. Since Q is quite often dated earlier than Mark, this thesis can then be pressed further to the notion that the Jesus of the Q community is the most authentic reflection of the Historical Jesus (who should thus be seen as primarily a sage), with the Markan Jesus being a later mythologization, perhaps due to the influence of the Pauline churches. It should be emphasized that none of this automatically follows from adopting the 2DH, and that many able advocates of the 2DH disown seeing Q in this way. It is nonetheless the case that this (some may say unorthodox) view of early Christianity collapses altogether if there never was a Q.

The view we take of the Synoptic Problem also affects how we understand the work of the Evangelists. The FH Luke who substantially reworks and reorders Matthew would seem to be a rather different kind of author from the 2DH Luke who largely confines himself to alternating blocks of Mark with blocks of Q interspersed with L (material unique to Luke) without making much of an effort to impose his own order on his result. The method of redaction criticism, which tries to understand an Evangelist's particular viewpoint on the basis of how he adapted his sources, clearly depends on deciding what his sources were. We can tell quite a lot about Matthew's concerns, say, by looking at the kinds of changes he tends (fairly consistently) to make to Mark, but our conclusions will be woefully awry if in fact Mark used Matthew. On the 2DH we can also make judgments about how Matthew adapted Q, and what that might tell us about Matthew's point of view, but if Q never existed, such judgments will be ill-founded.

Finally, different solutions to the Synoptic Problem imply different views of the Evangelists' working methods which may in turn suggest subtly different views on the Evangelists' individual aims and how their compositions should be understood.

You may have noticed the potential for all kinds of circularity here. Our preferred solution to the Synoptic Problem may affect the dates we assign to the various Gospels, but it could be that our preferred dating will influence our view of the Synoptic Problem. Our understanding of how the Evangelists worked may well affect our assessment of the viability of competing Synoptic source hypotheses, but our preference for a particular source hypothesis will inevitably affect our understanding of how the Evangelists worked. And while a particular solution to the Synoptic Problem may well affect our view of the Historical Jesus and the development of the Jesus tradition, our views on these questions may equally influence our decision to prefer one solution to another. This circularity is not exactly vicious, but it does indicate that the view we take on one point may be intimately bound up with the view we take on others, and hence with our overall view of how all these matters fit together.

To avoid getting tangled up in this potential circularity, we shall conduct our arguments here primarily from the internal evidence of the text; i.e., we shall be looking for the hypothesis that best explains what we find in Matthew, Mark, and Luke without much reference to any potential external evidence apart from that which gives us a general understanding about how other ancient authors went about their business. But before diving into any arguments, we should first review some of the realities of first-century text production.

2

Gospel Writing in the First Century

How Ancient Writers Worked

IF YOU TO TRY to picture the Evangelists at work writing their Gospels, what do you see? I can't read your mind, but it may be you imagine Luke sitting at his desk with copies of Mark and either Q or Matthew open in front of him, along perhaps with various other notes, sources and perhaps a copy of the Old Testament so that he can refer to them all at need as he pens his own composition. But just about everything in this picture would be wrong, not least because writing desks weren't used as early as the first century. For that matter, what we call the Old Testament wouldn't have been a single book bound between two covers that would neatly sit on anyone's non-existent desk, but a large collection of individual scrolls, which would be fairly cumbersome to keep referring to even assuming Matthew, Mark, or Luke had access to a complete set of them.

Even if Luke did have copies of his sources to hand, they would not be as easy to refer to as modern printed books. The Christian church was quicker than the surrounding culture to adopt the codex (the book format we're all familiar with, separate leaves bound between covers), but it's unclear whether they did so as early as the first century, and Luke's copies of Mark and Q or Matthew could well have been on scrolls (long rolls of papyrus or parchment which a reader would have to wind with one hand and unwind with the other to progress through the text). Either way, the text would be laid out in narrow columns, all in capital letters, with no spacing between words and minimal punctuation. At a first approximation, the effect would be something like this:

THEBEGGININGOFTHEG OSPELOFJESUSCHRISTS ONOFGODASITISWRITT ENINISAIAHTHEPROPHE TBEHOLDISENDMYMES SENGERBEFOREYOURF ACEWHOWILLPREPARE YOURWAYAVOICECRY INGINTHEWILDERNESS PREPARETHEWAYOFTH ELORDMAKESTRAIGHT HISPATHSITCAMETOPA SSJOHNWASBAPTIZING INTHEWILDERNESSAND PROCLAIMINGABAPTIS MFORTHEFORGIVENESS	OFSINSANDTHERECAM EOUTTOHIMALLTHERE GIONOFJUDEAANDALL THEJERUSALEMITESAN DTHEYWEREBAPTIZED BYHIMINTHEJORDANRI VERCONFESSINGTHEIR SINSANDJOHNWASCLO THEDINCAMELHAIRAN DALEATHERBELTAROU NDHISWAISTANDEATIN GLOCUSTSANDWILDHO NEYANDHEWASPROCL AIMINGSAYINGTHEREC OMESAFTERMEONESTR ONGERTHANITHEWHOS	SANDALTHONGSIAMNO TWORTHYTOSTOOPDO WNANDLOOSEIBATPIZE DYOUWITHWATERBUTH HEWILLBAPTIZEYOUWI THHOLYPSPIRITANDITC AMETOPASSINTHOSEDA USTHATJESUSCAMEFRO MNAZARETHOFGALILEE TOBEBAPTIZEDINTHEJO RDANBYJOHNANDIMME DIATELYCOMINGUPOUT OFTHEWATERHESAWTH HEAVENSRENTAPARTA NDTHESPIRITDESCENDI NGTOHIMLIKEADOVE

To be sure, this is not an exact representation. Apart from the fact that a first-century gospel manuscript would have been handwritten in Greek, not printed in English (here, my own rather literal translation of Mark 1:1–10), the columns would have been taller and probably a little narrower, and with slightly more visual aids for the reader (such as some rudimentary punctuation, marginal annotations, and perhaps indentation or spacing at key divisions in the text). Moreover, first-century readers (especially those literate enough to go about writing a Gospel) would have been far more comfortable than we are with reading texts in this format. It would not have been difficult for Luke (say) to have read through a copy of Mark laid out like this, particularly if he was already familiar with Mark's Gospel and vocalized the text as he went along. What would have been trickier, however, would be to locate particular passages in the text out of sequence (although ancient readers clearly could do this if they needed to). It would have been even more difficult to locate parallel passages in Mark and Matthew in order to compare them, especially where the order of passages in the two Gospels diverged. "Difficult" does not equate to "impossible," but if you try to imagine yourself scrolling through two different manuscripts to locate similar stories to compare them, for example, the Healing of the Paralytic in Matthew and in Mark, without the benefit of chapter and verse numbers or headings to help you, you can imagine why this might not be your preferred method of working.

Let's paint a picture of how someone like Luke is more likely to have worked. He won't have had a writing desk, but it's unlikely that he would have acted as his own scribe; ancient authors usually preferred to dictate. So we should imagine him sitting or perhaps standing, dictating to a scribe seated on a stool with a scroll, notebook, or waxed tablet (slats of wood covered with wax which can be inscribed on with a stylus) resting on his (or possibly her) knees. This would leave Luke's hands free to handle any written sources, but he is unlikely to have attempted to handle more than one at any one time. He will most likely have known all his sources reasonably well, and for much of the time he will probably have preferred to rely on his memory rather than consulting a manuscript. For his principal sources, such as Mark and Matthew (or Q), and perhaps some of his own special material (such as a collection of parables that appear only in Luke), he may have refreshed his memory by reading a section of one of his sources before starting to dictate his own version of that section. Where two sources (such as Mark and Matthew) ran conveniently in parallel (because Matthew had followed Mark's sequence) Luke might perhaps have refreshed his memory of both before composing his own version. It is unlikely, however, that Luke would have consistently maintained eye contact with any physical manuscript while composing. We should instead imagine him arranging his material in his head and then dictating it from memory.

It is possible that Luke made some notes of his own before beginning his own composition and that he might have consulted these notes from time to time. For the most part, though, he is more likely to have relied on his memory for most of his additional material. Ancient authors were far readier to rely on their memory than modern ones, and anyone undergoing a literate education (which Matthew and Luke must have done to at least some degree) will have been trained to memorize substantial amounts of material.

While Mark's Gospel reads as if it might have been a first draft dictated to a scribe, it is likely that Matthew and Luke would have polished their first drafts before "publication" (or that the secretaries to whom they dictated will have done this for them when they transcribed the text from notebook to scroll or codex). We can't be sure that this happened, since we don't know what resources were available to the Evangelists, and neither secretarial assistance nor writing materials would have come cheap to people on modest incomes, but it could well be that the Evangelists' church communities provided volunteer scribal labor for free and clubbed together to cover the cost of materials. Gospel writing may well have been a rather more communal effort than modern authorship tends to be.

This communal effort may have begun before the process of composition. The Evangelists may have been commissioned to write by their communities. They will most likely have discussed what they planned to write with fellow church members and received feedback about their efforts along the way. We should not imagine Matthew and Luke working from source material (such as Mark) they had just recently happened upon; it is more realistic to suppose that they had been familiar with their sources for quite some time, had discussed them with fellow believers, had perhaps been in the habit of reading them aloud for their congregations (whose members would have mostly been unable to read them for themselves), and perhaps either preached on and taught from them or had heard them being preached and taught from. For example, when Luke tells us that he had followed everything closely from the beginning (Luke 1:3) he should most probably be taken as meaning that he had for some time been thoroughly steeped in the tradition he was now going to write about.

"Publication" would also have been something of a communal process. In the absence of a printing press, copies had to be made by hand. Ideally an author might like to exercise some control over the process by issuing a master copy of the version of the text he considered definitive, but the reality is likely to have been messier. People may have jumped the gun by making unauthorized copies of early drafts, or by producing their own texts on the basis of what they'd heard read aloud. The Evangelists, or copyists further down the chain of transmission, may have taken the opportunity to improve on earlier versions of their text when fresh copies were made. We have no way of knowing whether the earliest distribution of the Gospels in the first century was supply driven or demand driven, that is, whether the Evangelists actively sought to disseminate their works by having copies made to send to other churches in the hope that they would then do the same, or whether other churches asked for other copies and perhaps sent their own scribes to make them. Most probably it will have been some combination of both.

We cannot be sure that the process sketched above corresponds precisely to the writing of the Gospels, but it is likely to be a good deal closer to how the Evangelists went about their work than how we might naively imagine it based on the way we do things today. Other models (or at least, variants of the model just sketched) are possible. If you'd like to go into these issues further, you could refer to my book *Writing the Gospels: Composition and Memory*.

Transforming Sources

Discussions of the Synoptic Problem often talk about the Evangelists copying their sources. In some passages the wording is so similar that it indeed looks as if at least one of the Evangelists must have copied their source (for example, compare what John the Baptist says at Matt 3:7–10 and Luke 3:7–9, or the very similar accounts of the Last Supper at Matt 26:26–29 and Mark 14:22–25). But even in these cases the wording is not exactly the same in the two Gospels being compared, and in others it diverges rather more (for an extreme example compare the Parable of the Talents/Pounds at Matt 25:14–30 and Luke 19:11–27). In general, it's quite misleading to speak of one Evangelist *copying* the work of another, since the Evangelists usually made at least some changes to the material they took over. This was the normal practice. Elite ancient authors generally strove not to reproduce the wording of their sources but rather to rework them to make their compositions their own. Writers further down the social scale (as the Evangelists appear to have been) may have been less scrupulous about this; it is notable how much of the wording the Evangelists are prepared to take over from their sources compared with the normal practice (or at least, normal elite practice) of the day. Nonetheless, none of the Synoptic Gospels straightforwardly copies any of the others (if it had, it would simply have been another copy of the source Gospel, not a new Gospel in its own right).

The differences between parallel accounts in the Gospels is often described in terms of redaction (i.e., editing), and for many purposes this may be reasonable enough. But for our purpose it risks being as misleading as "copying," since it may lead to a "copy and edit" view of composition that has more in common with the way in which we might edit a source text (open on our desk or our computer screen and then edited with pencil or keyboard and mouse) than the way in which ancient authors worked. Even where the Evangelists took over quite a lot of their source's wording, they should be understood as composing their own work, albeit doing so by reworking—and sometimes very closely reworking—their source.

Anyone capable of writing a gospel must have gone through at least some sort of literate education, even if only up to a secondary level (without, that is, having progressed to a full tertiary education in rhetoric). This secondary stage almost certainly included some work with *progymnasmata*, preliminary exercises aimed at equipping future writers and orators with the rudiments of composition. These taught the student various techniques for handling source material, such as paraphrase, precis, expansion, and elaboration (adding material to supply what might be missing in expression or thought). They were also taught how to handle various types of material such as chreiai (short anecdotes about a named individual often culminating in a pithy saying or deed), fables (of which the Gospel parables are a recognizable subtype), narrative, speech in character (that is, composing a speech appropriate to the speaker and the occasion), and ecphrasis (description). These are all techniques we can see used in the Gospels.

Ancient authors were much less likely to attempt close conflation at either the micro or the intermediate level. That is, they did not generally compare parallel accounts to combine individual words or phrases from each source, or even to reconcile the different details offered in each account into a single storyline. Rather, an ancient author would more typically choose which account to follow for any particular incident and then make that the basis for his own account, while perhaps incorporating the odd additional detail remembered from other accounts or background knowledge. Likewise, when using two or more sources ancient authors tended to follow any one given source for several pericopae (short sections) at a time, rather than skipping back and forth between sources after each pericope (pronounced pe-*ric*-oh-pee, and not to be confused with a submarine's viewing apparatus).

This doesn't mean that no conflation ever occurred at all. A measure of simple conflation might occur when, as we have seen, an author relying on memory brought in details recollected from another source. The appearance of conflation might also arise accidentally in two other ways. First, where an author was composing his own account from his memory of two very similar parallel accounts (on the 2DH, Matthew using Mark and Q where they overlap, say, or on the FH Luke using Matthew and Mark), his memory of one might interfere with his memory of the other, leading to a text that combined features of both. Second, where an author had become thoroughly familiar with the style and phraseology of one of his sources, he might become capable of composing a kind of pastiche that looks a little like a combination of different passages from that source (Matt 4:23—5:1, the introduction to the Sermon on the Mount, may have been composed in this way on the basis of Matthew's familiarity with Markan summaries). But none of these types of conflation is the same as deliberately combining individual words and short phrases from two or more accounts into one's own composite; it is this kind of deliberate micro-conflation that is uncharacteristic of ancient authors (and thus unlikely to have been attempted by the Evangelists).

It is debated just how far ancient authors were prepared to reorder their source material. On any theory of Synoptic relations at least two of the Evangelists must have done so to at least some extent, and it is apparent that other ancient authors did so as well. Different types of material are likely to have been treated differently. The sequence of events in a narrative might be rearranged to make the story flow better or to emphasize different events while maintaining the broader storyline. The sequence of sayings material might be arranged to create a different topical arrangement (for example, Matthew apparently rearranged many of Jesus' sayings into a number of set-piece discourses such as the Sermon on the Mount). It might also be rearranged to give certain sayings a different slant by placing them in new contexts. Rearrangement might also be aimed at rhetorical effectiveness, not least for speeches, for which guidelines existed on what kind of material ought to appear at different points. Such considerations become particularly relevant in the case of the Double Tradition (material common to Matthew and Luke but not found in Mark), which is mainly speech material, often arranged quite differently in the two Gospels in which it is contained.

The reordering of source material may have been constrained by the writing technology available. Given the format of an ancient scroll, or even an ancient codex, it could quickly become cumbersome to hunt through a source looking for a saying here and an incident there to incorporate into one's own composition in a different place. No doubt something could be achieved with rough notes on scraps of papyrus or waxed tablets, but these would not be nearly as easy to manipulate as index cards or the pages of a modern notebook (let alone text on a computer).

Having good memory command of one's source or sources would help, but it is unclear how much reordering could be accomplished in unsupported memory alone, in part because there is a single-figure limit on how many chunks of information human brains can keep in working memory at any one time. Random direct memory access to individual items in a substantial text is unproblematic: people reasonably familiar with the Bible today have little difficulty recalling the Lord's Prayer or the first beatitude or the basic storyline of the parable of the sower without having to look any of them up, and ancient authors would have been even more adept at this sort of thing. But the Evangelists would need to do more than pull a few items out of their original contexts; they would need to rearrange and often recontextualize a substantial body of material. Some people with highly trained memories could (and probably still can) perform quite prodigious feats of memory, which might enable them to range over a text in memory at will, pulling out items in any required order. But it would be perilous to assume that the Evangelists were memory virtuosi of this sort. The task becomes easier if the source material is arranged in a logical (narrative or topical) sequence that aids retrieving it from memory and also if the sequence into which it is being arranged has a reasonably clear logic of its own, so that one way to gather up material to be reordered from a source might be to perform several forward sweeps through that source.

It's doubtful whether we can determine what the Evangelists' memory could achieve by appealing to the psychology of memory or to our own intuitions. Quite apart from anything else, there are too many unknowns: all sorts of things can act as memory cues that might prompt recall, and ultimately we have no way of knowing what memory associations existed in the minds of the Evangelists (for all we may hazard the odd guess). Ancient authors clearly were capable of employing material in sequences that differed from those of their sources (Philo does so in many of his treatments of material from the Pentateuch, for example). Given that none of the Evangelists would need to have reordered their source material solely on the basis of their unsupported memory on the first attempt it is probably safe to assume that any rearrangement required of the Evangelists on any of the theories being considered here would have been possible for them given some combination of memory, notes, help from collaborators (not least the scribe taking dictation) and the production of more than one draft. We shall return to the question of order at more length in chapter 5.

Another question is whether there were any further techniques available to ancient authors beyond those we have just considered. One possible answer lies in the widespread use of literary (or rhetorical) *imitation*, in which authors might exhibit their skill and originality by reworking a well-known original or originals in a way that went well beyond mere reproduction. Such imitation might be of style, structure, content, themes, or some combination of all of these. A particularly salient example is the way in which Virgil's *Aeneid* imitates Homer's *Iliad* and *Odyssey*. Virgil's protagonist, Aeneas, combines elements both of Homer's Achilles (who takes part in a series of battles against his people's enemies) and Homer's Odysseus (who undergoes various adventures, including storms, shipwrecks, and encounters with potentially ensnaring women as he sails around the Mediterranean). At a broad-brush level, the *Aeneid* follows the structure of the *Odyssey* and then the *Iliad*. At a more detailed level, Virgil's use of Homer is more complex, combining elements of both epics into single incidents and characters in his own, and splitting others over multiple incidents and characters (for example, elements of Achilles are reused in both Aeneas and his arch-enemy Turnus, who in turn ends up in the role of Homer's Hector). While both the *Odyssey* and the *Aeneid* concern what happens to their respective heroes in the aftermath of the Trojan War, Virgil reshapes the material into the prequel to a grand drama looking forward to the rise of Rome and the reign of the Emperor Augustus. There is at least some parallel here to the way in which the New Testament makes use of the Old.

That the Gospels quote, allude to, and echo the Old Testament is not in doubt. In places they may also imitate it in ways at least partly analogous to Virgil's imitation of Homer (for example, the story of the raising of the widow of Nain's son at Luke 7:11–17 could be seen as an imitation of the raising of the widow of Zarephath's son at 1 Kgs 17:17–24, also alluded to at Luke 4:26). Dennis MacDonald (a New Testament scholar with a particular interest in literary imitation) has made a plausible case that the account of a storm and shipwreck at Acts 27:1—28:10 is (at least in part) an imitation of various storms and shipwrecks in the *Odyssey* (on the basis both of the course of events and on the occurrence of Homeric vocabulary in this section of Acts; although MacDonald's attempts elsewhere to see widespread imitation of Homer throughout Mark and Luke often appear rather less convincing). If Luke was prepared to imitate the Old Testament and Homer, perhaps he sometimes did the same with his other sources (in relation to content if not always style).

An imitation generally aimed at also being an emulation, namely a reuse of the imitated source that rivalled the original by aiming to at least equal if not improve on it. More generally, authors who adapted their sources using any of the techniques we've been looking at weren't simply making changes for the sake of making changes (although they might often be concerned not to be seen to be copying their sources too closely). In one way or another, they would be aiming to improve on their original. The improvements aimed at might be mainly stylistic (such as more elegant phrasing, better narrative flow or topical arrangement, or greater rhetorical effectiveness), but they might also be what we might broadly term ideological, that is to transform the account into something that better expresses the new author's beliefs or the needs of his target audiences or the requirements of a changed situation.

Aims, Genre, and Artistic License

Why would anyone in the first century write a gospel? There were no printing presses or mass literacy and to begin with the church got on perfectly well preaching about Jesus through word of mouth. But committing the story of Jesus to writing nevertheless had certain advantages. For one thing, in a culture in which literacy was limited and written texts far less pervasive than printed (and electronic) ones are today, a written text carried more symbolic weight and authority than something spoken (a vestige of that perception survives today, for example when people speak of giving more credence to something they see "set down in black and white"). For another, writing down one's own version of the story of Jesus helped to preserve that particular version in a more stable form than could be readily achieved by word of mouth; it also helped to disseminate that form of the story to a wider audience, since, once copies of a written gospel had been made and distributed, all that was needed to perform the version of the Jesus story was a copy of the gospel and someone with the ability to read it out aloud. While manuscripts and competent readers might be relatively rare, they would have been a good deal more common than persons trained to recite a gospel accurately from memory (as well as being far more likely to be around for a lot longer).

The mere passage of time may also have encouraged the writing of the Gospels, together perhaps with some precipitating crisis such as the Jewish Revolt and the consequent destruction of Jerusalem and its temple in 70 CE. As Jesus' first followers began to die out and authoritative eyewitnesses started to become thin on the ground, there would be an increasing need to preserve Jesus traditions for future generations. Committing some of those traditions to writing would have increasingly come to be seen as the best way to achieve this. Once one written Gospel existed, a precedent would have been set for others to follow. Anyone who wished to improve on or compete with an existing written Gospel will have had to produce a written Gospel of their own.

But the Gospels were never intended as purely archival, simply preserving facts about a figure of the past for the sake of satisfying historical curiosity. The Gospels rapidly came to serve as cultural texts, that is, texts that helped to shape and guide the communities for which they were written. They were probably intended for this role from the start. As cultural texts they would have both normative and formative functions. They would both provide guidance on how Jesus' followers should live (through the teaching and example of Jesus) and an account of how the Jesus movement came into being, to help give subsequent Christian communities a sense of identity: where there had come from, why they were there, what they stood for, and where they were going. The Gospels are stories that illuminate who Jesus was, why he remains so important, and what following him entails.

These are broad aims that all the Evangelists most likely had in common, but they would also have had more specific ones related to the needs of their target audience and their own perspectives on the significance of Jesus and the proper shape of Christian existence. So, for example, Matthew appears to have been a Christian Jew, quite likely from a scribal background, who was primarily addressing other Christian Jews who were becoming increasingly alienated from non-Christian Jews. As a Christian Jew addressing fellow Christian Jews, Matthew appears particularly anxious to show how Jesus' followers are the true heirs to the promises given to Israel and the true observers of God's Law, as well as demonstrating that Jesus was the true fulfillment of Israel's hopes. Luke, on the other hand, appears to have been writing primarily for gentile (non-Jewish) believers who saw themselves as being distinct from historic Israel. While Luke is as keen as Matthew to present the church as the true heirs of Israel, he presents the gentile church as a new community that is separate from Israel and has largely replaced it as God's people and is no longer bound by the Jewish Law. Matthew writes to legitimate and strengthen a group of Christian believers who see themselves as still belonging to Israel; Luke writes to legitimate and strengthen a different group who see themselves as quite separate.

Although the Gospels' genre has long been debated, there has been a growing consensus in recent years that the Gospels are best understood as *bioi* (lives), the ancient equivalent of biographies, that is, writing focused on the life, words, and deeds of a given individual. A *bios* (life) differed from a modern biography in several ways: it was not concerned to trace its subject's (emotional, intellectual, ethical or any other kind of) development; it did not have to be arranged chronologically; and it permitted greater artistic license than would be acceptable today. The aim of a *bios* was not simply to provide information about a figure of the past, but to present that figure as an example to be emulated (or perhaps avoided). The subject's character would be revealed, not through submitting him (most ancient *bioi* concerned men) to any kind of psychological analysis, but through a series of anecdotes thought to be revealing of his character, and through an account of his most notable deeds and (in the case of a figure like Jesus) sayings. *Bios* was a flexible genre, and the Gospels sit comfortably within it (although Luke's Gospel also forms part of a two-volume work that is perhaps better classified as history). That said, the Gospels also represent a particular sub-type of *bios*, distinctive not only in terms of their subject matter but also in their close orientation to the Jewish Scriptures.

Both ancient *bioi* and ancient historiography were genres that were meant to be factual (unlike, say, epic poetry or ancient romances). Someone writing a *bios* or history would be understood as making factual claims about the past. But not every ancient author was equally scrupulous in sticking to the facts, and in a culture where documentary evidence might be relatively scarce, it wasn't always easy to check the facts or to sift them successfully from rumor, fabrication, and stories that had grown in the telling. Moreover, ancient authors were allowed considerably more artistic license in their supposedly factual narratives than modern ones are. It was, for example, regarded as perfectly acceptable to alter details or change the order of events to bring out what one saw as their significance or to create a smoother narrative. Variations between parallel narratives in the gospels often lie comfortably within the scope of such artistic license; for example, the matter of whether Jesus encountered a blind man while he was leaving Jericho (Mark 10:46) or entering it (Luke 18:35), or indeed, whether he came across two blind men (Matt 20:29–30).

What is less clear is how far the Evangelists extended this artistic license. A comparison of the three Synoptic Gospels suggests that, whatever the relationship between them, their authors generally displayed considerable fidelity to their sources. But there are notable exceptions that appear to indicate a willingness to exercise considerable creativity on occasion, not least if we compare, say, Luke's account of the rejection at Nazareth or the call of the first disciples (Luke 4:16–30; 5:1–11) with their equivalents in

Mark and Matthew (Mark 6:1-6; 1:16-20; Matt 13:54-58; 4:18-22). Some proponents of the 2DH (such as F. Gerald Downing) tend to grant the Evangelists (especially Luke) rather less creativity and license than advocates of the FH, not least because in particular instances the plausibility of Luke's use of Matthew turns on how much license and creativity we're happy to attribute to Luke. It may be that we can't completely escape circularity here, but the two examples just cited (where on the 2DH Luke would presumably have been using Mark) arguably tip the balance in favor of allowing Luke more license than some proponents of the 2DH are comfortable with.

Scribal Copying

Until Johannes Gutenberg first produced a printed Bible in 1455, every manuscript of the Gospels was copied by hand. The scribes who made copies of the Gospels did so with varying degrees of care and professionalism, but no two manuscripts were ever completely identical, and in the first couple of centuries or so rather less care and control was likely to have been exercised than occurred later.

There are various reasons why copyists might depart from the texts being copied. Often it may simply have been due to error. A scribe could not maintain eye contact with the manuscript being copied at the same time as inscribing the copy. His or her eyes would have to continually switch between the two, relying on short term memory to transfer a few words at a time. Every now and again that memory might err, or the scribe might go back to the wrong place in the source text. Or scribes copying a text with which they were already very familiar might tend to rely on their memory of that text, which might be less than perfect. Or a scribe who was familiar with one Gospel (Matthew, say) might inadvertently introduce some of that Gospel's wording when copying a similar passage from a less familiar Gospel (Luke, say).

In addition to these accidental errors, scribes might also introduce deliberate changes, aiming to "improve" the text either by attempting to correct what they took to be the errors of previous copyists or by tweaking the text to make it say what they thought it ought to say (perhaps in the belief that was what the Evangelist in question must have meant), sometimes just to make sense of a puzzling text but often in the interests of what the scribe perceived to be doctrinally correct. The vast majority of textual variants do not materially affect the sense of the Gospels (or other books of the New Testament), although a few are quite significant. But they can become more important where an argument turns on the precise wording of parallel passages, as often happens when evaluating competing solutions to the Synoptic Problem.

Given that the earliest production of Gospel copies may have been relatively uncontrolled, many textual critics cast doubt on the very notion of an "original" text of any of the Gospels. The most that text criticism can aim at is to arrive at a form of the text that is most likely to be the ancestor of all surviving texts, but this can only be pushed back as early as the second century at best. It follows that the one thing we can be sure of is that the Gospel texts printed in our modern Bibles are identical neither to what the Evangelists wrote nor to any Gospel texts they may have uses as sources. Neither will any two Evangelists have worked from precisely the same text of any common source; thus, for example, unless Matthew and Luke used the same physical manuscript of Mark (which is highly unlikely), they will have been using texts of Mark that differed to some degree.

This clearly creates difficulties for arguments that rely on the exact wording of parallel texts. If Matthew, Mark, and Luke all agree in a particular case, is that because Matthew and Luke both decided to take over Mark's wording unchanged, or is it because the subsequent process of copying tended to assimilate the wording of all three Gospels at that point? If Matthew and Luke agree against Mark, does that indicate that Luke knew Matthew, or that a copyist has assimilated Luke's wording to Matthew's, or that Luke and Matthew used a text of Mark that differed from ours?

The difficulties should not be exaggerated, however. The tendency to assimilate the texts of the three Synoptic Gospels was not sufficient to eradicate their individual characteristics. Often there are no significant textual variants that need to be taken into account. Even where significant textual variants exist, there are often reasonably strong text critical grounds to prefer one reading over another, even if certainty is impossible. The existence of textual variants is something we should be aware of, but it should not be allowed to paralyze us. In particular, if the aim of any proposed solution to the Synoptic Problem is to provide the most economical hypothesis that fits the surviving evidence, then it is reasonable to take "the surviving evidence" to refer to the texts of the Gospels as textual criticism is best able to reconstruct them, while allowing that there will be a few cases of genuine uncertainty and that variations between the texts of different copies of the

Gospels constitute one further reason why any source-critical theory can only hope to approximate to what actually took place.

Consequences for Models of Synoptic Relationships

The points covered in this chapter further underline why any model of synoptic relationships (at least any model that is straightforward enough to be useful) can only be a model, hopefully a reasonable approximation to what may have occurred, but hardly a full account of everything that resulted in the texts of the Gospels as we now have them. To recapitulate, here are some of the principal factors that we cannot fully take into account because the relevant evidence is no longer available and because the processes involved would in any case be too complex to be fully manageable:

1. The continuing existence of oral tradition and of individual and communal memory alongside that of written sources.

2. The possible (but by no means certain) use of other lost written sources, including but not restricted to private notes.

3. The use made of oral and written sources (for example, for preaching, teaching, discussion, and debate) in the Evangelists' communities prior to their writing their Gospels (and the ways in which such uses influenced the Evangelists' compositions).

4. The extent of collaboration between the Evangelists and other people in their communities in the process of composition (for example, feedback offered on early drafts and suggestions made by colleagues with whom the Evangelists discussed their work or by the scribes to whom they dictated).

5. The ways in which the different Evangelists' memories interacted with these various factors, and the associations existing in each Evangelist's memory.

6. The possibility that (at least some of) the Gospels went through several drafts (or at least one preliminary draft followed by subsequent polishing) before being issued for copying, and that even after copies started to be made, the Evangelists or their associates continued to revise their texts.

7. The changes made to the texts of the Gospels in the course of copying them, the degree of cross-contamination from the text of each Gospel to that of the others, and the precise form of the texts available to the Evangelists as sources.

In order to keep the discussion manageable, in what follows we shall proceed largely as if these complications were only marginal. That is (in common with many arguments over the details of the Synoptic Problem) we shall largely argue as if the Gospels were principally the products of single authors relying mainly on known written sources for all the material they share with those known written sources, as if the Evangelists arrived at the final version of their Gospels more or less at the first attempt, and as if the first-century texts of the Gospels were pretty much the same as the text of our modern critical editions. These assumptions are sufficiently shaky that from time to time we'll need to keep one eye on the kinds of complicating factors listed above, but for the most part we'll take it that they are not so distorting as to undermine our attempts to evaluate competing models.

3

The Two Document Hypothesis

Overview

THE TWO DOCUMENT HYPOTHESIS (2DH) maintains (1) that Mark was the first Gospel to be written; (2) that Matthew and Luke made independent use of Mark; and (3) that in addition Matthew and Luke made independent use of a second source (commonly designated Q). At a first approximation, Mark accounts for the so-called Triple Tradition (TT) material in Matthew and Luke, and Q for the so-called Double Tradition (DT) material (material shared by Matthew and Luke but not found in Mark). These distinctions are not quite as neat as they appear because (1) Matthew has quite a bit of material shared with Mark but not Luke and Luke a small amount of material shared with Mark but not Matthew; and (2) the 2DH is obliged to postulate the existence of some material shared by Mark and Q, the so-called "Mark–Q overlaps," which are then a kind of hybrid of the Double and Triple Traditions.

This leaves a fair amount of material that's unique to Matthew and unique to Luke. You'll often see these bodies of material referred to as M and L. Unfortunately, these terms are not always used consistently. Particularly in some older scholarship on the Synoptic Problem, notably in the Four Source Hypothesis propounded by B. H. Streeter, M and L were taken to be further documentary sources employed by Matthew and Luke respectively. The existence of these additional documentary sources has now largely fallen out of scholarly fashion; these days the symbols M and L are more often used to denote Matthew's and Luke's special material without implying anything about where it came from. But M and L can also refer to the stream of tradition (perhaps a mix of oral and written) thought to lie behind the material unique to Matthew and Luke. On the Farrer Hypothesis (FH) there is no reason to draw a sharp distinction between M and Q. It may be left as an exercise to the interested reader to work out what becomes of M and L on other theories, such as the Two Gospel Hypothesis (2GH) or Matthean Posteriority Hypothesis (MPH—Matthew using Mark and Luke). In what follows M and L will be used in a purely descriptive sense to designate material that's unique to Matthew and Luke respectively.

In this chapter we'll proceed in three stages. First, we shall examine the case for Markan Priority. Second, we shall set out the reasons why the 2DH sees the need for Q. Third, we shall examine these standard arguments for Q and try to show that they are not nearly so compelling as they are often taken to be.

Markan Priority

Belief in Markan Priority (i.e., that Mark was the first of the Synoptic Gospels to be written and was subsequently used by the other two) is shared by the 2DH, FH, and MPH. While not everyone accepts it, it is probably the aspect of the Synoptic Problem on which there is widest agreement.

We saw some initial reasons for supposing that Mark came first back in chapter 1. It is the shortest of the three Synoptic Gospels and is roughly coextensive with the material shared by all three. Mark's order nearly always agrees with either Matthew's or Luke's (and often with both), and his wording agrees with Luke's and Matthew's more than Matthew's does with Luke's. This would seem to suggest that Matthew and Luke both expanded Mark with additional material of their own, not least stories about Jesus' birth and infancy and resurrection appearances, which are lacking in Mark (most modern scholars believe that Mark originally ended at Mark 16:8) along with a substantial amount of teaching material, which Mark has rather less of.

Seeming to suggest is not, however, the same thing as proving. Proponents of the 2GH (who believe Mark came last) would argue that Mark's order results from Mark having deliberately reconciled that of Matthew and Luke. The agreement in wording between the Gospels is explained by Mark's carefully conflating the wording of Matthew and Luke. On this scenario, Mark would be aiming both at a short, fast-paced dramatic account potentially suitable for performance at one sitting and for one that mediates between the Jewish-facing Matthew and the gentile-facing Luke.

Stated at this level of generality, the 2GH case seems reasonable. Showing how it falls apart under closer examination provides at least indirect support for Markan priority.

First, while it was not uncommon for ancient authors to abbreviate a source to produce an epitome (a kind of Reader's Digest version), they did not generally do so by attempting to abbreviate two sources in combination or by omitting some incidents and expanding on others (in many incidents shared between all three Gospels, such as the Gerasene demoniac and the epileptic boy, Mark contains a substantially longer account). It's true that Mark's account is sometimes the shortest, most strikingly so in the temptation story, but there it becomes hard to explain why Mark should have taken what was essentially the same story in both his sources and cut it so drastically to produce an almost cryptically brief account.

Second, it is also unclear why someone wishing to reconcile Matthew and Luke should have omitted so much of what they had in common, such as the Lord's Prayer and the infancy and resurrection narratives. Luke and Matthew have different versions of these, but surely Mark could have chosen one or the other or else have attempted to produce his own version based on both (as the 2GH supposes he did elsewhere).

Third, it is curious that an order that results from mechanically reconciling those of two occasionally conflicting sources should give every appearance of being a structure devised by Mark that makes sense on its own terms.

Fourth, it is also odd that if Luke used Matthew and Mark used both, Matthew and Mark end up agreeing in wording with each other against Luke rather more than Luke does with Matthew against Mark.

Fifth, the close conflation of Matthew and Luke that Mark would need to have carried out is uncharacteristic of the way in which ancient authors typically worked (as we saw in the previous chapter). While we cannot say such conflation would have been impossible for an ancient author, the format of the manuscripts Mark would have been working from would certainly have made it difficult enough for him to have needed a very powerful motive to attempt it. Moreover, Mark is the least literary of the three Synoptic Gospels; a Mark who can write such unsophisticated Greek and yet carry out such a complex and sophisticated literary operation seems hard to imagine.

That Mark's Greek is less literary than either Matthew's and Luke's suggests rather that Mark came first and that the other two sought to improve on his Greek. While is not impossible that someone could write less well than their sources, ancient authors usually attempted to improve on their source material. Mark's Greek is close to the register of oral narration; that this should result from Mark's literary use of more literary sources seems odd, while Luke's and Matthew's improvement of Mark's Greek from a more oral to a more literary register is closer to what one would expect. We may illustrate this by comparing the way in which Mark and Matthew describe the call of the first disciples.

Mark 1:16–20	Matthew 4:18–22
And going along by the sea of Galilee he saw Simon and Andrew the brother of Simon casting their nets in the sea; for they were fishermen. And Jesus said to them, "Come after me, and I will make you become fishers of people." And straightway leaving the nets they followed him. And going on a little he saw James the [son] of Zebedee and John his brother and them in the boat mending the nets. And straightway he called them. And leaving their father Zebedee in the boat with the hired servants they departed after him.	Now, walking along by the sea of Galilee he saw two brothers, Simon called Peter and Andrew his brother, throwing a casting-net into the sea; for they were fishermen. And he says to them, "Come after me, and I will make you fishers of people." So, leaving their nets immediately, they followed him. And after going on from there they saw two other brothers, James the [son] of Zebedee and John his brother, in the boat with Zebedee their father mending their nets, and he called them; so after immediately leaving the boat and their father they followed him.

I've translated both extracts as literally as possible both to bring out the differences in style and to make it easier to see the similarities and differences between them. It's worth noting in passing the similarities in wording between these two accounts (see if you can spot them all), this illustrates why it is likely that there is a literary relationship between them. What we're more concerned with here, however, are the differences. One that's particularly striking is the way that Mark starts nearly every sentence with "and" (the technical name for this is *parataxis*). Matthew has less of this. Note how Matthew also takes more care over how he introduces the two pairs of brothers. The distinction between Mark's εὐθύς (*euthus*—"straightway") and Matthew's εὐθέως (*eutheōs*—"immediately") may be less apparent here; a broader comparison between the two Gospels would show that Mark tends to use "straightway" much more frequently, even when it served as

The Two Document Hypothesis

little more than a connective, whereas Matthew employs "immediately" more sparingly, as a true adverb. Here he wants to emphasize the impact of Jesus' authoritative call by highlighting the disciple's instant response. Overall, Mark is closer to an oral style of narration, while Matthew shows greater literary sensibilities, for example by varying his connectives and crafting his sentences with more care. While one might be able to imagine a scenario in which it made sense for Mark to turn Matthew's more carefully crafted prose into his more oral style of narration, it would be hard to find many first-century parallels to anyone doing this to a source, and it is much easier to envisage Matthew polishing Mark's cruder effort.

A further argument in support of Markan priority is the incidence of editorial fatigue. Despite what the name may suggest, this does not refer to an editor becoming tired, but rather to the user of an earlier text starting out by changing it in certain ways but not carrying the changes through consistently (the "fatigue" referred to is thus a form of inadvertence). Where oddities in one text look like the result of editorial fatigue in relation to another, this forms a good indicator of the direction of dependence.

A few examples should illustrate how editorial fatigue favors Markan priority. Mark's version of the Healing of the Paralytic (Mark 2:1-12), has the paralytic's four friends carry him to Jesus on a stretcher. Since the crowd around Jesus prevents them from getting to Jesus through the door, they climb up onto the roof, dig through, and let the paralytic down through the roof on his stretcher (Mark 2:3-4). Their determination apparently makes a positive impression on Jesus, since Mark at once goes on to say, "And having seen their faith Jesus says to the paralytic . . ." The parallel at Matt 9:2-8 says nothing about anyone climbing onto the roof and letting down the stretcher, but merely records that people carried the paralytic to Jesus on a bed; yet Matthew still remarks on Jesus' seeing their faith. Which is easier: to suppose that Matthew started off abbreviating Mark but left in the remark about Jesus seeing the stretcher-bearers' faith (although it's no longer clear what this refers to), or that Mark came across Matthew's account, found the comment about Jesus seeing people's faith puzzling, and so added the detail about roof excavations to account for it? No doubt one could try to make a case either way, but which seems more plausible?

For a second example, we may compare how Mark and Matthew narrate the request for the brothers James and John to be given the places of honor (at Jesus' right and left hand) when Jesus comes into his kingdom. In both Gospels, Jesus has just predicted his forthcoming crucifixion in Jerusalem (Mark 10:32-34 || Matt 20:17-19), so that the request comes at an egregiously inappropriate moment. In Mark, it is James and John who make the request (Mark 10:35-37) and it is to James and John that Jesus then naturally addresses his reply (Mark 10:38-40), leading to indignation at James and John from the other ten disciples (Mark 10:41). In Matthew, however, the inappropriate request is made by James's and John's mother (Matt 20:20-21), although Jesus proceeds to answer the brothers just as if the request had come straight from them (Matt 20:22-23) and the other ten disciples are once again indignant with James and John (Matt 20:24). Their mother is mentioned nowhere else in the passage; it is as if she appears out of thin air just to make her request and disappears back into thin air before Jesus can answer it. It thus looks as if Matthew introduced the mother into the story to spare having her two sons make such a blatantly self-serving request but then failed to carry through the logic of this change, which in turn suggests that he must have been reworking an account that looked very much like Mark's.

For an example of editorial fatigue in Luke, we may compare Luke's account of the feeding of the five thousand with Mark's. According to Mark, this takes place in a "desert place" to which Jesus has just withdrawn and to which the crowds follow him (Mark 6:32-33 || Matt 14:13). Luke, however, has Jesus and the disciples withdraw to "a city called Bethsaida" (Luke 9:10b-11). But in all three Gospels the disciples tell Jesus to send the crowds into the neighboring villages and countryside to buy food, because they are in a "desert place" (Mark 6:35-36 || Matt 14:15 || Luke 9:12). This fits the setting in Mark (and Matthew), but hardly fits Luke's setting (Bethsaida, which Luke describes a city—*polis*). Luke thus appears to have started out adapting an account that looks very much like Mark's but failed to carry through his changes consistently.

Such examples could be multiplied, but these serve to illustrate the point. There are several instances where an apparent oddity in Matthew or Luke can readily be explained on the assumption that they were adapting Mark but failed to do so consistently, but which are harder to understand if Matthew and Luke were composing independently of a prior account. One might manage to come up with a reasonably plausible explanation of how the different versions ended up the way they are on the basis that Mark came last, but the question is then which direction of dependence seems the most likely in practice? While Mark's use of Matthew or Luke in such cases is not demonstrably impossible, it does appear to go against the grain compared with Luke's and Matthew's editorial fatigue in adapting Mark.

The same principle extends to all the arguments we have just been considering. In isolation any of these arguments for Markan priority could be countered with a proposal why the direction of dependence could be the other way around (that is for why, contrary to initial appearances, Mark could have used Matthew and/or Luke). But in none of the instances we have examined is such a counter-proposal particularly compelling, and in each of them Markan priority seems the more natural choice, and when all the arguments are taken together, any case against Markan priority starts to resemble a possibly valiant but ultimately doomed attempt to swim against a particularly powerful current. Markan priority is not thereby proved beyond the possibility of any reasonable doubt whatsoever, but it nevertheless emerges as by far the most plausible option.

The Case for Q

The Two Document Hypothesis (2DH) and the Farrer Hypothesis (FH) agree that Mark was the first of our Gospels to be written, but disagree on the need for an additional source "Q" to account for the material shared by Matthew and Luke but not found in Mark (the so-called Double Tradition or DT). Given that no copy of Q has ever been found and no ancient author refers to anything that we can plausibly identify as Q, it may seem odd to propose the existence of such a document in preference to the seemingly simpler solution that Luke derived his DT material from Matthew (or Matthew from Luke). Proponents of the 2DH do not, however, insist on the need for Q just because they like conjuring up mysterious lost sources, but because they believe that Luke's use of Matthew (or Matthew's of Luke) raises too many difficulties to be plausible, which leaves Luke's and Matthew's independent use of Q as the next simplest option.

Although we shall be arguing that this belief is mistaken, it is far from arbitrary; the 2DH deserves to be taken seriously not just because it has been the dominant Synoptic source critical theory for the last century and a half but because it has some serious arguments to offer. In this section we shall summarize these arguments; in the next we shall question whether they are as cogent as commonly supposed. Without further ado we shall now list the five principal arguments against Luke's use of Matthew and two subsidiary arguments for the existence of Q.

1. *The Argument from Order.* Matthew and Luke diverge both in the order and the context of the DT material almost everywhere after the Temptation Story. Since Luke reorders Mark less aggressively than Matthew does (especially in Matthew chapters 8–9), it is assumed that Luke broadly follows the order of Q. On the 2DH Luke thus alternates between his two main sources, Mark and Q (or sometimes, Q + L, where L means the material unique to Luke) in a simple manner resembling the way in which other ancient authors frequently worked, while on the FH he breaks up Matthew's discourses, such as the Sermon on the Mount, and scatters their contents into less obviously appropriate contexts (much of it across his long central section). His motivation for doing this seems less than clear, and it would be difficult to achieve with first-century writing technology (for example, if we have to envisage Luke winding through his scroll of Matthew to hunt down odd bits and pieces to assemble into some quite different order).

2. *Alternating Primitivity.* It is (according to this argument) sometimes Luke and sometimes Matthew that has the earliest version of some saying, which means (it is said) that neither can have used the other (since the direction of dependence would then have to be both ways at once). Thus Matthew and Luke must each have used a common source (Q). Examples commonly given in support of this argument include the Lord's prayer, in which Luke's shorter version (Luke 11:2–4) is said to lack Matthew's liturgical elaborations (Matt 6:9–13) and the Beatitudes, in which, for example, Luke's simpler "Blessed [are you] poor" (Luke 6:20) is clearly (it is said) more primitive than Matthew's spiritualized version, "Blessed [are] the poor in spirit" (Matt 5:3). A more generalized version of this argument might be renamed *Redactional Plausibility*, applying to instances in which it appears difficult to see why Luke would have changed Matthew the way FH Luke would have to have done. (Examples where Matthew appears prior to Luke could also be given, but since the 2DH is usually concerned to argue against Luke's use of Matthew, the examples most commonly cited tend to be ones where Luke's version is said to look more primitive.)

3. *Infancy and Resurrection Narratives.* Although Matthew and Luke agree in adding Infancy and Resurrection narratives to Mark's account (which is believed to have originally ended at Mark 16:8 with the women fleeing in terror from the empty tomb), their infancy and

resurrection narratives look entirely different. This seems hard to explain if Luke was using Matthew (or Matthew using Luke). In Matthew, Joseph and Mary are natives of Bethlehem who flee to Egypt to escape Herod's jealous infanticide, and only settle in Nazareth after Herod's death to avoid the jurisdiction of Herod's son Archelaus. In Luke, Joseph and Mary are natives of Nazareth who happen to be visiting Bethlehem on account of an imperial census when Jesus is born and then return home to Nazareth without having attracted any threat or notice from the authorities at all. In Matthew, Jesus' principal resurrection appearance takes place on a mountain in Galilee, while Luke's Gospel records a number of resurrection appearances in and around Jerusalem, the last of which is an ascension from the Mount of Olives.

4. *Matthean Additions to Mark Missing from Luke.* The 2DH asks, if Luke used Matthew, why doesn't he take over Matthew's additions to Mark? Despite the way this argument is sometimes incautiously phrased, proponents of the 2DH are well aware that quite a few of Matthew's additions to Mark do appear in Luke, so what the objection really amounts to is, why doesn't Luke take over *more* of Matthew's additions to Mark than he appears to have done on the FH? Why, for example, does Luke not take over the conversation between Jesus and John the Baptist (Matt 3:14–15) or Jesus' enthusiastic response to Peter's Confession (Matt 16:17–19) or Pilate's handwashing and his wife's dream (Matt 27:24, 19)?

5. *Unpicking.* In certain passages, notably many of the so-called Mark–Q overlaps (where, on the 2DH, the same incident or saying appears in both Mark and in Q, with Q having the fuller version), it is claimed that Luke would apparently have had to go out of his way to avoid what Matthew had closely in common with Mark, while further modifying what Matthew modified from Mark and taking over unchanged what Matthew added to Mark. On the face of it this "unpicking" of Matthew from Mark would be both pointless and difficult to achieve (given the format of ancient manuscripts). It is thus highly implausible to suppose that Luke would have attempted such an unprecedented technique for adapting his sources; it is far more likely that in such cases Matthew combined Mark and Q while Luke simply followed Q.

Two subsidiary arguments sometimes offered are more relevant to the nature than to the existence of Q, although the first could apply to both.

6. *The Coherence of Q*. Q as reconstructed turns out to be a coherent text (a quasi-narrative introduction followed by a series of speeches on various topics). This indirectly supports the existence of Q (since it appears to be a coherent document and not just a ragbag of sayings), but also points to the nature of Q (as a single document).

7. *Wording and Order*. In places the wording of Matthew and Luke in the Double Tradition (DT) is so close as to make a literary relationship between them virtually undeniable. Moreover, while Matthew and Luke differ in the contexts in which they place most of their DT material, there is quite a bit of agreement in the relative order of the Double Tradition in both Gospels (that is, once extracted from its Matthean and Lukan contexts, much of the DT from both Gospels follows much the same order). Taken together, these two features of the DT strongly suggest that it is taken from a single document. If we have ruled out the possibility that that single document could be either Matthew or Luke, then it must be Q, and Q in turn must be a single document and not some amorphous collection of sundry texts and oral traditions.

A full defense of the Two Document Hypothesis would spell out these seven arguments in more detail and support them with many more examples, and perhaps add a few further (though most probably lesser) arguments into the bargain, but the summary just provided gives a good enough indication for now of the main arguments that have persuaded many scholars of the need for Q.

But Is Q Necessary?

The arguments listed in the previous section appear to make a good case for Q. Even if I end up persuading you that the Farrer Hypothesis provides a better solution to the Synoptic Problem, it's important that you gain some appreciation of the strength of its main rival. There are good—or at least seemingly good—reasons why so many scholars have adhered to the Two Document Hypothesis and you need to be aware of them. Now, however, we shall question how good these reasons actually are. We'll address each of them in turn.

The Argument from Order

This argument is sufficiently weighty that it merits a chapter to itself, so we shall return to it more fully in chapter 5. One preliminary point may nevertheless be made straight away. That is that the argument from order does not give the 2DH as much an advantage over the FH as it may seem. If Luke largely follows the order of Q, then it is indeed the case that 2DH Luke has an easier job of simply alternating blocks of Mark and Q than FH Luke has of alternating blocks of Mark and substantially reordered Matthew. But the advantage to 2DH Luke comes at the cost of an equal disadvantage for 2DH Matthew. Since the order of Q is supposed to be (pretty much) Luke's order, any difference between the order of the Double Tradition in Luke and Matthew must reflect the same difference between the order of the same DT material in Q and Matthew, so that whatever reordering of DT material FH Luke would need to have performed on Matthew, 2DH Matthew would need to have performed in reverse on Q.

Alternating Primitivity

This argument asserts that there are places where Luke's version of a saying looks more primitive than Matthew's, so that Luke cannot have derived it from Matthew. But this argument only works if everyone agrees that Luke's version *is* clearly the more primitive. Yet all too often this is a matter of subjective judgment backed up by little solid argument, as if the mere assertion that Luke's version is clearly the more primitive were sufficient to establish it as fact.

This assertion can readily be challenged in two of the most commonly cited examples that some defenders of the 2DH come perilously close to regarding as virtually self-evident: the Lord's Prayer and the Beatitudes. First the Lord's Prayer as it appears in Matthew and Luke.

Matthew 6:9b–13	Luke 11:2–4
Our Father who [is] in the heavens; Hallowed be the name of you; Come be the kingdom of you; Done be the will of you; As in heaven also on earth.	Father, Hallowed be the name of you; Come be the kingdom of you;

Matthew 6:9b–13	Luke 11:2–4
Our bread for sustenance give us today,	Our bread for sustenance keep giving us day by day.
And forgive us our debts, As also we forgive those indebted to us.	And forgive us our sins, For we also ourselves forgive all who are indebted to us.
And do not bring us into testing, But rescue us from evil [*or*, from the evil one].	And do not bring us into testing.

These highly stilted translations are intended to reproduce some of the poetic flavor of the underlining Greek. For example, the three lines ending "of you" near the start of Matthew's Lord's Prayer represents the repeated line ending -*ma sou* (σου—"your"), while the oddly phrased "Hallowed be ... Come be ... Done be ..." is an attempt to echo the underlying Greek *hagiasthētō ... elthetō ... genethētō* (ἁγιασθήτω ... ἐλθέτω ... γενηθήτω) with its internal rhyme at the start of these three lines.

It is often asserted that Luke's version of the Lord's Prayer is self-evidently more primitive because it is shorter and simpler, while Matthew's version shows evidence of liturgical elaboration. Yet the relative primitivity of the Lukan Lord's Prayer is far from self-evident. Even in the English translation given above, Matthew's version of the prayer looks more poetic than Luke's. The kind of poetic features Matthew's Prayer employs are precisely the characteristics that help make something memorable and hence better fitted to survive in oral transmission. There's a reason why it's Matthew's version of the Prayer that people know today. Moreover, the features of Matthew's Prayer that scholars point to as being due to liturgical elaboration are (as most would acknowledge) much the kinds of thing that would be typical of other Jewish prayers that survive from around this time. So, which is more likely to be the more primitive version, the briefer one, or the more poetic one better suited for oral transmission and better resembling the sort of thing one would expect from a Jewish milieu? As we saw in chapter 2, students in antiquity were taught both to expand and to abbreviate their sources; shorter is not automatically earlier, and it's at least as possible that Luke abbreviated the Prayer to suit his gentile audience as that Matthew expanded it for his Jewish one.

One further indication points to Matthew's version being the more primitive. Where Matthew has "And forgive us our debts as we also forgive those indebted to us" Luke has "And forgive us our sins for we ourselves also forgive all who are indebted to us." Matthew reflects an underlying

Aramaic idiom in which the word for "debt" can be used to mean "sin." Luke apparently changes "debt" to "sin" for the benefit of his gentile target audience, who may not be familiar with this idiom, but then retains Matthew's "those indebted to us," a possible sign of Lukan editorial fatigue with respect to Matthew.

These considerations may not prove beyond all reasonable doubt that Luke derived his version of the Lord's Prayer from Matthew's, but they cast serious doubt on the assertion that Luke's version must be the more primitive one.

The other common example of Luke's supposedly obvious primitivity compared with Matthew is constituted by the Beatitudes where, it is said, Matthew has clearly spiritualized Jesus' blessings on the literally poor and literally hungry that Luke has preserved from his source. But once again, this is far from being anything like as self-evident as is commonly supposed.

As is well known, Luke is particularly exercised by the themes of wealth and poverty. Faced with Matthew's "Blessed [are] the poor in Spirit" (Matt 5:3a) Luke may well have written "Blessed [are] the poor" (Luke 6:20b) to reflect this interest. Luke, unlike Matthew, adds a series of woes to balance his Beatitudes, for example, "But woe to you the rich" (Luke 6:24a). Not only does this show Luke's concern to contrast literal poverty with literal wealth, it also makes it hard to see how the woe could have been worded had the corresponding Beatitude retained Matthew's "in spirit": "But woe to the rich in spirit"?

It's also worth noting that Luke's contrast between the rich and poor, replete and hungry in his version of the Beatitudes and Woes strongly echoes Luke's Magnificat: "He has put down the powerful from their thrones and exalted the humble; he has filled the hungry with good things and sent the rich away empty" (Luke 1:52–53).

Thus, even if Jesus did in fact utter the words "Blessed are the poor" and Matthew was responsible for adding "in spirit" (although we have no way of knowing that for sure), it would be entirely in line with Luke's own interests for him to have omitted Matthew's addition when he came to compose his own version.

None of this demonstrates that Luke *must* have derived his version from Matthew, but we have shown that he may plausibly have done so, and that is all that is needed to undermine the alternating primitivity argument.

Infancy and Resurrection Narratives

In the next chapter we shall argue that Luke may owe rather more to Matthew's infancy and resurrection accounts than is generally acknowledged, making them potentially more problematical for the 2DH than the FH. But we may offer a few preliminary observations here.

Luke's Gospel is followed by a second volume, the Acts of the Apostles, which opens with Jesus' disciples still in Jerusalem and told to remain there until Pentecost (Luke 24:49; Acts 1:4–5). This is theologically important to Luke, allowing him to both begin and end his Gospel in Jerusalem (with close associations to the temple) and to summarize what is to come in Acts as the spread of the gospel "in Jerusalem, and in all Judea and Samaria, and unto the end of the earth" (Acts 1:8). Luke may also have thought it more plausible historically that the disciples remained in Jerusalem throughout the period from the Resurrection to the coming of the Holy Spirit at Pentecost, not least on the basis of the traditions he presumably drew on for the early chapters of Acts. That being so, Luke could not have taken over Matthew's appearance story (set on a mountain in Galilee—Matt 28:16–20) unchanged. Luke's willingness to amend his sources for such reasons is in any case demonstrated by his treatment of the empty tomb story at Mark 16:7, where Mark's "he [Jesus] is going ahead of you into Galilee; there you will see him" becomes "Remember what he said to you when you were in Galilee . . ." (Luke 24:6); Luke has altered Mark to suppress the expectation of a resurrection appearance in Galilee.

Luke may also have regarded Matthew's infancy narrative as historically dubious, either because he recognized it as being strongly based on the stories of Moses and Israel in the Old Testament or because his own traditions indicated that Jesus' family had been natives of Nazareth all along. Be that as it may, the opening of the Gospel was the place for Luke to set out his stall, just as it was for the other three Evangelists, and Luke's stall clearly differed from Matthew's (or Luke would not have bothered to write a Gospel of his own). Put differently, Luke will have wanted to use his infancy narrative to introduce the main themes that he would then develop in his two-volume work (Luke–Acts), and Luke's emphases differed from Matthew's (as we briefly discussed in the previous chapter).

Finally, the differences between Luke's and Matthew's infancy narratives need to be accounted for on any theory of synoptic relations. If we suppose that Luke's narrative is different because he relied on a different source, then he may well have preferred that source to the version he found in Matthew. If, on the other hand, we suppose that Matthew and Luke each developed a common source in very different ways, then it is hard to imagine what such a source must have looked like to give rise to such seemingly different accounts (given that they also have some features in common). The appeal to such a hypothetical source would be in danger of simply disguising the problem by pushing it back from Luke's use of Matthew to Luke's use of some unknown X, which may as well have been Matthew if it also gave rise to Matthew's account. Yet to suppose that Matthew's and Luke's versions each grew independently through a long process stemming from a few common traditions is to ignore the ways in which the Matthean and Lukan infancy narratives cohere thematically to the extent they do both internally and with what follows in the respective Gospels (e.g., the theme of Jesus as New Moses in Matthew).

Matthean Additions to Mark Missing from Luke

The 2DH asks, if Luke used Matthew, why didn't he take over (more of) Matthew's additions and alterations to Mark? As posed this question presupposes either what is manifestly false (that Luke and Matthew share no common additions or alterations to Mark) or else something highly dubious (that there is some set quantity of Matthean additions and alterations to Mark that FH Luke should have taken over but in fact failed to).

Matthew and Luke share substantial additions (or substantial alterations) to Mark in a number of pericopae (passages) such as the preaching of John the Baptist, the temptation, the Beelzebul controversy, the mission discourse and the parable of the seed growing secretly. These are the "Major Agreements" of Matthew and Luke against Mark. Virtually everyone recognizes not only their existence but the need for a literary explanation to account for them. On the 2DH that explanation is that these passages occur in both Mark and Q (so-called "Mark–Q overlaps") so that the common additions can be explained by Matthew's and Luke's use of Q. While this may save the 2DH from terminal embarrassment, it does not negate the fact that on the Farrer Hypothesis these are passages where Luke did take over Matthew's additions to Mark.

A further set of Matthean modifications shared by Luke are provided by the so-called minor agreements, which are far more numerous though individually less impressive. We shall be looking at some of these more closely in the next chapter. Suffice to say here that they provide a further, and potentially very sizeable set (perhaps in the order of a thousand) of agreements of Matthew and Luke against Mark, which might reasonably be taken as evidence of Luke's taking over Matthew's changes to Mark.

The 2DH complaint then turns on Luke's failure to take over a number of Matthean additions to Mark that he had no obvious reason to reject; the examples we gave above were the conversation between Jesus and John the Baptist (Matt 3:14–15), Jesus' enthusiastic endorsement of Peter's confession (Matt 16:17–19), and Pilate's handwashing and his wife's dream (Matt 27:24, 19). It is unclear how we can be sure that these are additions Luke *ought* to have taken over, but two points become relevant here. The first is that, in common with the way most ancient authors typically worked, we should suppose that FH Luke will have followed one source at a time. Most of Luke's alleged failures to take over Matthew's additions to Mark occur in passages where FH Luke was most likely following Mark, without direct reference to Matthew. Although Luke may have brought in the occasional change he happened to remember from Matthew, it's unreasonable to expect him to have done so in any systematic fashion. That Luke does not take over Matthew's changes to Mark in these cases is thus principally the result of his primarily using Mark in these passages.

The second point is that a relationship between two texts is established by what they have in common, not by what they do not. If you were accused of plagiarizing someone else's work in your essay, a single sentence in common would suffice to convict you of the charge; it would do no good to point to all the material you hadn't stolen from your source. Similarly, if Luke were to stand accused of plagiarizing Matthew, the charge would be proved on the basis of the material they shared (in this cases their common changes to Mark); Luke would not escape the charge by pointing to all the Matthean additions to Mark he hadn't taken over.

Unpicking

The unpicking argument concerns the implausibility of Luke's "unpicking" Matthew's additions to Mark in certain passages where there are substantial agreements of Matthew and Luke against Mark. It is far from clear, however, that this is what Luke would have to have done. On the Farrer Hypothesis, in the passages in question (the Major Agreements, aka Mark–Q overlaps) Matthew will have modified and added to Mark, while Luke will have modified Matthew without conscious reference to Mark (beyond the odd reminiscence). If one author modifies another's work and then a third modifies the second, it is unsurprising if the third writer's version diverges from the first more than the second one does. Moreover, since the passages in question are ones in which Luke has chosen to base his own account on Matthew's rather than Mark's, it is also unsurprising that Luke should reflect more of the account he preferred than the one he did not.

The parable of the mustard seed provides perhaps the most straightforward example of this.

Mark 4:30-32	Matthew 13:31-32	Luke 13:18-19
And <u>he was saying</u>: "How shall we liken **the kingdom of God** or in what parable are we to put it? As **a seed of mustard**, which when it is sown on the ground, being *smallest of all the seeds* on the ground, and when it is sown, it comes up and becomes *the greatest of* all the *shrubs* and makes large branches, so that under its shade **the birds of heaven** can **nest**.	Another parable he put before them saying: "**The kingdom of** the heavens is like a seed of mustard, <u>which a man took</u> and sowed in his field. It is the *smallest of all the seeds*, but when it *grows it is the greatest of shrubs* and becomes a tree, so that **the birds of heaven** come and **nest** in its branches.	So <u>he was saying</u>: "What is **the kingdom of** God <u>like</u> and to what shall I liken it? It is like a seed of mustard which <u>a man took</u> and threw into his garden. It g<u>rew and became a tree and </u>**the birds of heaven** <u>nes</u>ted <u>in its branches</u>

The clumsy English translation is designed to bring out the similarities and differences in the underlying Greek. Bold type indicates where all three Gospels agree, italic type where Matthew otherwise agrees with Mark, plain underlining where Luke otherwise agrees with Matthew, and wavy underlining where Luke otherwise agrees with Mark.

The 2DH "unpicking" objection to the FH here is that FH Luke would have rejected what Matthew took over from Mark (the contrast between the tiny mustard seed and the large plant into which it grows), while retaining Matthew's principal change to Mark (that the seed grows into a tree in whose branches the birds build their nests). But rather than suppose that Luke unpicked Matthew's additions to Mark in this way, it is (the 2DH maintains) simpler to suppose that Luke represents the Q version of the parable, which Matthew has combined with the Markan version. Otherwise we must suppose that Luke carefully compared Matthew and Mark just so he could avoid what they had in common, which would be an utterly bizarre thing for him to have done.

But this description of FH Luke's procedure here is simply false. The words in bold indicate where Luke has taken over what Matthew shares with Mark; these might be phrases without which the parable could hardly be told, but they are nevertheless similar in extent to the Markan material Luke has not taken over from Matthew; there is no systematic effort here by Luke to avoid Matthew's Markan material just for the sake of it. On the contrary, Luke's introduction to the parable is more like Mark's than Matthew's is (unlike Matthew, Luke does not place it immediately after a series of other parables, so Matthew's introduction would be inappropriate). Luke leaves out the comparison between the smallest of seeds and greatest of shrubs because it is irrelevant to the point he wishes the parable to make (against the synagogue leader who has just carped about his healing a crippled woman on the sabbath; the benefits of the Kingdom are not to be restricted in the way Jesus' critics suppose).

Conversely, if Luke's version of this parable is taken straight from Q, then Matthew must have closely conflated Mark and Q in a way uncharacteristic of ancient authors. It is 2DH Matthew, not FH Luke, who follows a problematic procedure here.

In chapter 4 we shall encounter a more complex example of alleged unpicking (the Beelzebul Controversy) in the course of discussing major agreements between Matthew and Luke.

The Coherence, Wording, and Order of Q

As previously stated, these are more in the nature of supporting arguments for Q once it has been established that Luke's use of Matthew is implausible on other grounds than primary arguments against the Farrer Hypothesis. We may nevertheless note in passing that on the FH, the apparent coherence of Q is not some fluky coincidence, but a consequence of the way it is reconstructed; what the 2DH calls Q is, on the FH, the result of Luke's selection and arrangement of the DT material he has taken over from Matthew; that it displays some marks of deliberate editorial activity is therefore to be expected.

While the extent of common wording and order in the Double Tradition may indeed suggest a relationship between documents, it could just as

The Two Document Hypothesis

well (and we shall shortly argue, better) indicate a direct relationship between Matthew and Luke as an indirect one mediated by a documentary Q.

In sum, the arguments the 2DH most commonly urges against Luke using Matthew turn out not to be nearly as compelling as they are commonly taken to be (although, to be fair, we have only skimmed the surface of this debate here; to do more would take us beyond the scope of a beginner's guide). The fact that we have needed to counter these standard 2DH arguments at all may give the impression that the FH has to swim heroically against just as strong a current as objections to Markan priority do, but the two cases are not the same, since the arguments that favor Markan priority are generally stronger than those opposed to Luke's use of Matthew. That said, some readers may feel we have now arrived at something of a stalemate, with neither the 2DH nor the FH managing to deliver a decisive blow to the other. To resolve this apparent stalemate, the next chapter will discuss some positive indications of Luke's use of Matthew that the 2DH may struggle to explain.

4

Luke's Knowledge of Matthew

Overview

THE PREVIOUS CHAPTER DISCUSSED the main reasons why many people suppose Luke could not have used Matthew and so find a need for Q. We found that on closer examination these reasons are not nearly as compelling as proponents of the Two Document Hypothesis (2DH) claim. The next step is to look at some similarities between Luke and Matthew that are hard to explain unless one of them did use the other.

We shall begin by examining the openings of these two Gospels, which resemble each other in ways that the 2DH might struggle to account for. We'll then look more briefly at the Gospels' endings, where the similarities are less striking but still sufficient to undermine the contention that Luke cannot have known Matthew. We shall next turn to the places where Matthew and Luke agree against Mark (the so-called major and minor agreements) to an extent that would be odd if Matthew and Luke were making independent use of Mark. Finally, we'll briefly explain why even in the Double Tradition—material the 2DH supposes Matthew and Luke independently took from Q—there are some passages that point to a more direct relationship between Luke and Matthew.

But we should first clarify three points. The first is that Q, as the 2DH defines it, has no infancy narratives and no passion or resurrection stories, so that any similarities that occur between Matthew and Luke in these parts of their Gospels cannot be explained by recourse to Q. The second is to reiterate that similarities count more than differences. That two different Gospels will differ is a statement of the obvious; Luke would not have bothered to write a Gospel of his own if he had been completely happy with Matthew and Mark. But even one telling similarity between Luke and Matthew (that their independent use of Mark and Q cannot explain) constitutes potential evidence of Luke's use of Matthew, and while one or two such pieces of potential evidence might be explained away as the result of coincidence (or textual corruption), the cumulative weight of many such similarities cannot be dismissed so lightly. The point remains even if Luke's reasons for changing what he found in his sources aren't always immediately obvious. The third point is that while Luke's use of Matthew does not automatically rule out his use of additional (oral, written, or memory) sources, it does mean that none of those sources can be Q (in the sense defined by the 2DH). Moreover, once we have established that Luke's use of Matthew (alongside Mark) is more probable than not, it is surely preferable to see how much can be explained by his use of these two (known) sources before invoking any hypothetical ones.

Beginnings

At first sight, the infancy narratives in Matthew and Luke look strikingly different. According to Matthew, Mary is found to be pregnant before being married, so that her future husband Joseph resolves to break off the engagement. He is prevented from doing so by the appearance of an angel in a dream telling him not to be afraid to take Mary as his wife, since her pregnancy is due, not to her intercourse with another man, but to the agency of the Holy Spirit, in fulfilment of a prophecy from Isaiah. After the birth, a group of magi (seers or astrologers) from the east follow a star to Judea. Arriving in Jerusalem they ask the reigning king, Herod, about the new king born in his realm. Herod consults his experts and learns the Messiah is to be born in Bethlehem. Herod accordingly sends the magi to Bethlehem to find the child and report back to him (ostensibly so he can pay him homage but in fact so he can eliminate the threat to his reign). The magi duly follow the star to Bethlehem, where Mary and Joseph have apparently been living all along, and present gifts to the child. Being warned by a dream, however, they return home by a different route to avoid encountering Herod again. Joseph is likewise warned in a dream and flees to Egypt by night, taking Mary and the infant Jesus with him. An infuriated Herod responds by ordering the massacre of all the male infants (up to two years old) in and around Bethlehem. After Herod's death, an angel appears to Joseph in yet another dream telling him to take the child and his mother back to the land of Israel, but on returning to Judea, Joseph finds that Herod's son Archelaus is now ruling in his stead, and so decides to settle in Galilee, which is how the holy family fetch up in Nazareth.

In Luke's story, Mary and Joseph lived in Nazareth all along. There are no magi, no guiding star, no massacre of children, and no flight to Egypt. Instead, Mary and Joseph travel from Nazareth to Bethlehem on account of an imperial census, and Mary gives birth while they're there. In place of a visit from exotic magi following a star from the east we have one from a group of nearby shepherds, guided by an angelic message. Shortly afterwards, Joseph and Mary take their newborn child to Jerusalem to present him to the Lord in the temple, and subsequently return home to Nazareth with the infant Jesus. Luke's opening chapter also contains a parallel story about the birth of John the Baptist to Mary's relative Elizabeth (nothing of which appears in Matthew). In contrast with Matthew's dark narrative in which the holy family become refugees from a ruler's bloodthirsty violence, Luke's narrative conveys an atmosphere of piety and rejoicing, with many of the characters bursting into spontaneous songs of praise that comment on events.

Yet while these stories are quite different on the surface, they also contain numerous similarities, many of which cannot readily be explained on the basis of common tradition. The most notable of these are:

1. Jesus was born in Bethlehem but raised in Nazareth.

2. Jesus' father was named Joseph (Matthew and Luke also agree that his mother was named Mary, but this would have been apparent from Mark 6:3).

3. Jesus was born during the reign of King Herod (i.e., Herod the Great).

4. After Jesus' birth, he and his parents were visited by a group of strangers in response to a sign pointing to his Messiahship.

5. Both accounts contain genealogies tracing Jesus' descent from David through Joseph (although the Davidic descent itself could have been inferred from Mark 10:47 and was in any case known to Paul: Rom 1:3).

6. Both accounts predict that Jesus is to be a savior (Matt 1:21; Luke 2:11).

7. In both cases the birth is announced in advance by an angelic messenger who stipulates that the child is to be called Jesus and that the Holy Spirit will play a role in his conception. In both cases this takes place while Mary is still a virgin betrothed to Joseph.

8. Luke and Matthew both suggest that Joseph plays no role in Jesus' conception.

Further detailed agreements emerge when we compare these two annunciation accounts more closely:

Matthew 1:18-25	Luke 1:26-38
And the birth of Jesus Christ was thus. After his mother Mary was betrothed to Joseph, before they came together, she was found to be pregnant from the Holy Spirit. But her husband Joseph, being a righteous man and not wanting to expose her, was willing to divorce her secretly. But while he was considering these matters, behold an <u>angel</u> of the Lord appeared to him in a dream saying, "<u>Joseph</u>, son of <u>David</u>, *don't be afraid* to receive <u>Mary</u> [as] your wife. For that which is begotten in her is from the <u>Holy Spirit</u>. And she will *bear a son and you shall call his name Jesus*; for he will save his people from their sins." Now this all happened in order to fulfil what was spoken by the Lord through the prophet saying, "Behold the virgin shall conceive and bear a son and they shall call his name Emmanuel," which, being translated, means "God [is] with us."	In the sixth month the <u>angel</u> Gabriel was sent from God to a city of Galilee named Nazareth to a virgin betrothed to a man named <u>Joseph</u> from the house of <u>David</u> and the name of the virgin was <u>Mary</u>. And when he had come to her, he said, "Greetings, favored one, the Lord is with you." But she was perplexed by this saying and pondered what kind of greeting it might be. And the angel said to her, "*Don't be afraid*, Mary, for you have found favor with God. And behold, you shall become pregnant and *bear a son and you shall call his name Jesus*. He shall be great and be called Son of the Most High and the Lord God will give him the throne of his father David, and he will rule over the house of Jacob forever and his kingdom will have no end." But Mary said to the angel, "How shall this be, since I do *not know* [i.e., I am not having sexual relations with] a man [or husband]?"
	And in reply the angel said to her, "The <u>Holy Spirit</u> shall come upon you and the power of the Most High shall overshadow you; and thus the holy begotten shall be called [the] son of God. And behold, your kinswoman Elizabeth has also conceived a son in her old age and this is the sixth month for her who is called barren; for with God every word is not impossible."
Then when Joseph arose from sleep, *he did as the angel of the Lord commanded him* and received his wife, and he did *not know* [i.e., have sexual relations with] her until she gave birth to a son; and he called his name Jesus.	And Mary said, "Behold the Lord's slave; *may it happen to me according to your word.*" And the angel departed from her.

In Matthew, an (anonymous) angel of the Lord appears to Joseph in a dream, while in Luke the angel Gabriel comes to Mary, but there are nevertheless several similarities between the two accounts:

1. The word "angel" followed by the names Joseph, David, and Mary occur shortly after one another in the same order in both accounts.
2. Both accounts contain commands not to be afraid (although they are expressed slightly differently in Greek and could be regarded as a typical feature of this kind of scene).
3. Both scenes concern Mary's unexpected pregnancy (although in Matthew, Mary is already pregnant while in Luke this apparently lies in the future).
4. Both accounts include a denial of sexual relations between Mary and Joseph, expressed in the biblical idiom of "knowing."
5. Both accounts associate Mary's pregnancy with the activity of the Holy Spirit.
6. In both accounts Jesus' birth fulfils a prophecy. This is explicit in Matthew, who cites Isa 7:14, but implicit in Luke, who paraphrases the promise made to David at 2 Sam 7:12–14a.
7. Both accounts prophesy that the child to be born will have a major role to play for his people.
8. Both accounts note the recipient's obedience to the angelic command.
9. Both accounts contain an identical string of seven Greek words: [τέξεται δὲ/τέξῃ] υἱὸν καὶ καλέσεις τὸ ὄνομα αὐτοῦ Ἰησοῦν (*texetai de/texē huion kai kaleseis to onoma autou Iēsoun*—"[she/you shall bear] a son and you [singular] shall call his name Jesus"). These words admittedly follow the pattern of similar formulas announcing forthcoming births in various Old Testament passages, but the similarity between Matthew and Luke nevertheless remains, and while "you shall call his name" fits the context in Matthew where it is addressed to Joseph, it is odder in Luke where it is addressed to Mary, since Luke elsewhere regards naming a child as the father's prerogative (Luke 1:59–63).

Taken together the density of these parallels strongly suggest a relationship between the two accounts. When these parallels are taken in conjunction with those previously noted (which partially overlap), the case for such a relationship becomes even stronger. If Luke did not use Matthew, they must instead have used a common source, but postulating a hypothetical common source only pushes the problem back a stage. If the source resembled Matthew, it may as well have been Matthew. If it resembled Luke, then Matthew's changes to it are no easier to explain than Luke's changes to Matthew would be. If it contained only what is common to both, it is hard to see how it could have constituted a coherent narrative. It is thus simplest to assume that Luke used Matthew. That Matthew's birth narrative fits in so well with other aspects of his opening, not least Matthew's temptation story, further strengthens the case for seeing Matthew as Luke's source for what the two have in common. (In brief, Matthew's temptation story continues the themes of Jesus recapitulating the stories of Moses and Israel that are set out in his infancy narratives).

There are yet more resemblances to come. Although Luke and Matthew may appear to go their own separate ways in their respective second chapters, the structures of their narratives continue to contain a remarkable number of similarities:

1. Events take place "in Bethlehem of Judea in the days of Herod the King" (Matt 2:1); "in the days of King Herod of Judea" (Luke 1:5).

2. Jesus is born in Bethlehem (Matt 2:1; Luke 2:4).

3. Visitors (magi/shepherds) are directed to the newborn Jesus by a sign in the heavens (Matt 2:1-2, 9; Luke 2:8-14), which is said to be an occasion for "great joy" (χαρὰν μεγάλην—*charan megalēn*, an unusual phrase found at both Matt 2:10 and Luke 2:10).

4. The magi/shepherds find Jesus and respond to him in a manner appropriate to what they have been told about him (Matt 2:9-12; Luke 2:16-17).

5. The magi/shepherds return to their starting place (Matt 2:12; Luke 2:20).

6. Joseph, Mary, and Jesus then go elsewhere (Matt 2:14; Luke 2:22).

7. Arguably, both the flight into Egypt and the presentation at the temple redeem Jesus' life at the cost of other lives (Matt 2:16; Luke 2:23-24).

8. Joseph, Mary, and Jesus subsequently settle down in Nazareth (Matt 2:23; Luke 2:39).

9. Both accounts suggest that Jesus' coming will upset the existing order and both foreshadow the deadly opposition Jesus will eventually encounter in Jerusalem (Matt 2:3–6; Luke 2:34–35; see also 1:51–54).

These parallels suggest that Luke is emulating Matthew's account by imitating many of its features while transforming many of them to better suit his own purposes. So, for example, Matthew's exotic foreign magi (μάγοι—*magoi*) are replaced by Luke's local shepherds, representatives of the humble poor outsiders whom Luke consistently presents as the beneficiaries of Jesus' ministry. The magi would have struck Luke as inappropriate persons to come and greet the Christ-child, both because it is too soon in the grand scheme of Luke–Acts for Jesus to be recognized by gentiles, and because Luke would have regarded magi as dangerously akin to magicians, of whom he disapproved; for example, see Acts 13:8 for Elymas the magician (μάγος—*magos*, the singular of *magoi*). The magi's expensive material gifts (of gold, frankincense, and myrrh) are replaced by the shepherd's words, which Mary finds precious enough to store up in her heart (Luke 2:17–19). More broadly, Luke replaces Matthew's dark tale of royal scheming, infanticide, and forced flight with an altogether brighter one with an emphasis on rejoicing among the poor and truly pious. At the same time, he elevates the status of Jesus' mother both by focusing more of the account on her and by downplaying Matthew's apparent admission that she conceived Jesus out of wedlock.

Luke clearly did employ the technique of literary imitation in his infancy narrative. It has long been observed that Luke's opening chapters are written in the style of the Septuagint, the Greek translation of the Old Testament. His infancy narratives also imitate OT content, drawing on various models, but chiefly on the opening of 1 Samuel. At a general thematic level, both the opening of Luke and the opening of 1 Samuel involve unlikely births that are to lead to the salvation of Israel. The prophet Samuel, who will eventually anoint David as king (1 Sam 16:13) corresponds to John the Baptist, who heralds the coming of the Messiah (i.e., Anointed One) from David's line. More specific correspondences between the early chapters of 1 Samuel and Luke include:

1. John the Baptist and Samuel are both born of mothers said to be barren, Elizabeth (Luke 1:7) and Hannah (1 Sam 1:5).

2. Elizabeth is married to a priest (Zechariah) who is serving in the temple, and to whom John's birth is first announced (Luke 1:13), while Hannah is visiting an earlier temple when Eli the priest promises that her plea for a son will be answered (1 Sam 1:16–17).
3. Hannah's response to Eli's promise (1 Sam 1:18) resembles Mary's response to the angelic annunciation (Luke 1:28, 38).
4. Hannah and Mary respond to events with similar songs of praise (1 Sam 2:1–10; Luke 1:46–55); while Luke draws on a number of OT models here, Hannah's song is the most significant.
5. The promise of a son to Mary and the declaration of his name (Luke 1:31) resemble the birth and naming of Samuel (1 Sam 1:20), although the precise formula Luke employs has closer parallels elsewhere (notably Gen 16:11 and Isa 7:14) and was presumably taken over from Matthew.
6. Hannah (1 Sam 1:11) and Mary (Luke 1:38) both identify themselves as God's δούλη (*doulē*—female slave or maidservant).
7. The presentation of Jesus in the temple (Luke 2:22–38), which does not reflect Jewish custom, may instead reflect the presentation of Samuel to the temple (1 Sam 1:22–28).
8. The boy Jesus makes an unscheduled stay in the temple after being accidentally left there by his parents (Luke 2:41–50) while the boy Samuel serves in the temple (1 Sam 3:1–18) having been left there by his parents (1 Sam 1:21–28); both boys outperform their elders while there.
9. Both Jesus (Luke 2:52) and Samuel (1 Sam 2:26) are said to have grown in stature and in favor with God and with people (see also Luke 2:40b and 1 Sam 2:21b).

These parallels are not all exact, but imitation is not copying, and often involves transformation of material taken over from the model. Such transformation can readily include the splitting and joining of roles borrowed from the model. It is thus no objection to Luke's imitation of 1 Samuel that he splits material from Samuel's infancy narrative over his own infancy narratives of John and Jesus. Moreover, Luke does not simply imitate the style of the Greek Old Testament here; his imitation extends to borrowing and adapting his content (perhaps because lacking any detailed tradition concerning the births of Jesus and John he proceeded on the assumption that God would have acted with them as he had in the past, resulting in a broadly similar pattern of events). The important point is that Luke's imitative use of 1 Samuel is similar to that we are arguing he made of Matthew. The composition of Luke's infancy narrative follows a consistent method.

The similarities between the openings of Matthew and Luke extend beyond their infancy narratives in ways that suggest Luke continued to use Matthew well into their respective fourth chapters (after which Luke switches to following Mark for a while). It would take too much space to argue that in detail here, so we shall simply list some of the more salient similarities.

1. Matt 3:3 and Luke 3:4–6 both truncate Mark's compound prophetic citation (Mark 1:2–3) in identical ways and move it to after John's initial preaching of repentance (Matt 3:1–2 || Mark 1:4 || Luke 3:2–3).

2. Matt 3:7–10 and Luke 3:7–9 add to John's preaching in virtually identical words, with a speech beginning "You brood of vipers." In Matthew this insult is addressed to the Pharisees and Sadducees whom Matthew consistently portrays as opposed to Jesus, whereas in Luke it is addressed to the crowds who have come to be baptized (which hardly seems to merit such vitriol). Luke thus looks secondary to Matthew here.

3. Matt 3:11c–12 and Luke 3:16c–17 further expand John's preaching in virtually identical words, beginning in mid-sentence with "and with fire" following the words "but he will baptize you with Holy Spirit" shared with Mark 1:8b. If Matthew and Luke shared any other source (such as Q) besides Mark here, it can hardly have begun with the words "and with fire," and so must have contained the substance of Mark up to that point. The 2DH explains this as a Mark–Q overlap, proposing that Q contained essentially the same material as Mark and then extending it in the same way as Matthew and Luke, but then at this point Q may as well be Matthew.

4. Both Matt 4:1–11 and Luke 4:1–13 expand the brief temptation narrative at Mark 1:12–13 with an account of the same three specific temptations, albeit with the order of the final two reversed between Matthew and Luke. The Matthean temptation narrative fits the Matthean context particularly well in continuing the Moses/Exodus/Israel theme

of Matthew's infancy narratives; like Israel, Jesus is tempted in the wilderness after passing through a body of water, and the first temptation involves hunger, just like Israel's first complaint after crossing the Red Sea. Like Moses, Jesus fasts for forty days and forty nights, and in replying to the tempter, Jesus three times cites Moses (in Deuteronomy). Matthew's second and third temptations then foreshadow what is to come later in his Gospel. "If you are the Son of God, throw yourself down" (Matt 4:6) foreshadows the taunt, "Save yourself, if you are the Son of God, come down from the cross" (Matt 27:40b). The third temptation, in which the devil takes Jesus to a high mountain to show him all the kingdoms of the world, which the devil will give him if Jesus will worship him (Matt 4:8–10), is ironically reversed in the closing resurrection appearance (Matt 28:16–20) in which Jesus is worshiped on a mountain and declares that all authority in earth and heaven has been given to him. The 2DH explains the temptation narrative as another Mark–Q overlap, but Q would seem to fit Matthew's purpose suspiciously well here. Moreover, the repeated "If you are the Son of God" of the temptations appears to presuppose something very like the declaration of Jesus' divine sonship at the end of the Baptism story (Matt 3:17b || Mark 1:11b || Luke 3:22b), causing some 2DH advocates to propose that Q must also have contained an account of the Baptism. Taken in conjunction with points 2 and 3 above, this starts to expand Q into something very like Matthew, and once that happens, we may as well say that Luke used Matthew.

5. The similarities between Luke and Matthew are less evident after their temptation narratives, but they continue to occur as far as Luke 4:30 (after which Luke switches to Mark for the story of the Capernaum demoniac). Luke's summary of Jesus' ministry at Luke 4:14–15 shares with Matt 4:23–24 the phrase διδάσκων/ἐδίδασκεν ἐν ταῖς συναγωγαῖς αὐτῶν (*disaskōn/edidasken en tais sunagōgais autōn*—"[he was] teaching in their synagogues," with "*their* synagogues" being characteristically Matthean). While Luke's account of Jesus' inaugural sermon at Nazareth (Luke 4:16–30) may well be his reworking of the rejection at Nazareth in Mark 6:1–6a, it also has several points of contact with Matt 4:13–16. Both passages mention Capernaum, both cite prophecies from Isaiah that are said to be fulfilled and are followed by Jesus' preaching, and both use the rare form Ναζαρά (*Nazara*) to refer to Nazareth (Matt 4:13; Luke 4:16). Luke moreover agrees with

Matthew against Mark in having Jesus travel from Nazareth to Capernaum following the temptation (Matt 4:13; Luke 4:30–31). While these similarities may not prove Luke's use of Matthew, they certainly suggest it, and cannot readily be accounted for by appeal to Mark–Q overlap.

Endings

We have already argued (in chapter 3) that Luke's need to keep Jesus and the disciples in Jerusalem prevented him from taking over Matthew's closing Galilean resurrection narrative (Matt 28:16–20). Yet while the resurrection accounts in Luke do not resemble those in Matthew as closely as their infancy narratives do, there are nonetheless enough similarities between the endings of Luke and Matthew to suggest possible contact between them.

1. Jesus' final appearance takes place on a mountain in both Matthew (28:16) and Luke (Luke 24:50 places it at Bethany, which Luke 19:29 locates on the Mount of Olives).

2. Both Matthew (28:17) and Luke (24:11, 24, 41) mention disciples' doubt or disbelief at Jesus' resurrection.

3. Both Matthew and Luke indicate that from now on Jesus will have both earthly and heavenly authority (Matt 28:18; Luke 24:51). Admittedly, this is explicit in Matthew but only implicit in Luke, where Jesus ascends into heaven to a position of authority at the right hand of God (Luke 22:69; Acts 7:56).

4. Both Matthew and Luke have Jesus commission the disciples for mission. At Matt 28:19 Jesus command his disciples to go and make disciples of all nations (πάντα τὰ ἔθνη—*panta ta ethnē*) baptizing them in the name (εἰς τὸ ὄνομα—*eis to onoma*) of the Father, Son and Holy Spirit, while at Luke 24:47 Jesus states that repentance and forgiveness of sins are to be preached in his name (ἐπὶ τῷ ὀνόματι αὐτοῦ—*epi tō onamati autou*) to all nations (πάντα τὰ ἔθνη—*panta ta ethnē*).

5. In both accounts Jesus makes a promise beginning with the words καὶ ἰδοὺ ἐγὼ (*kai idou egō*—"and behold I"). At Matt 28:20 the promise is that Jesus will remain with his disciples until the end of the age. At Luke 24:49 it is that they will be clothed with power from on high, in

other words the Holy Spirit, who substitutes for Jesus' ongoing personal presence in Acts.

6. In both accounts the disciples are said to worship Jesus (Matt 28:17; Luke 24:52 in some manuscripts).

Admittedly not all manuscripts of Luke contain all the parallels suggested above (the ending of Luke being particularly afflicted by textual variants, including some that might impact items 3, 5 and 6 above), so that this list of similarities could be reduced by opting for the least favorable readings in Lukan manuscripts. That said, the readings relied on above appear in the main text of modern critical editions of the Greek New Testament and so cannot simply be ruled out. There is some danger of some circularity here, in that adherence to a particular source-critical theory might influence one's text-critical decision on which readings to prefer: a belief that Luke either did know or could not have known Matthew might be part of one's reason for either accepting or rejecting the readings in question. The evidence is not always as unambiguous as we might like.

Moreover, while the parallels listed above are suggestive, many may feel that they fall short of demonstrating that Luke's resurrection accounts *must* have made use of Matthew's. Nevertheless, Luke's imitation of the opening of Matthew makes his imitative transformation of Matthew's ending that much more plausible. At the very least, Luke's independence from Matthew in the final chapter of Luke's Gospel is far from assured.

Major and Minor Agreements

Similarities between Luke and Matthew are by no means confined to their beginnings and endings. A surprising number of similarities also occur in the Triple Tradition, where, according to the Two Document Hypothesis, Matthew and Luke should be making independent use of Mark, but where Matthew and Luke often agree against Mark. These agreements are usually termed *major agreements* and *minor agreements*. These terms are less than ideal, both because the extent of Matthew/Luke agreements against Mark run along a continuous spectrum rather than falling into two neat groups, and because the term "minor agreements" may suggest something of only minor import. We shall nevertheless carry on speaking of major and minor agreements here, both because these terms are so often used in treatments of the Synoptic Problem, and because they provide a convenient way to structure our discussion.

The term "major agreement" is a less prejudicial way of referring to passages that the Two Document Hypothesis labels "Mark–Q overlaps," passages in which Matthew and Luke agree in adding a substantial body of very similar material to Mark. The term "substantial" is imprecise but means that Matthew and Luke share more than the odd word or short phrase that differs from Mark; major agreements sometimes extend to several sentences. While there is no precise boundary between major and minor agreements, in practice major agreements are those that most scholars feel point to some sort of literary relationship beyond Matthew's and Luke's use of Mark. On the FH this relationship is believed to be a direct one between Luke and Matthew; the FH holds that the major agreements come about where Luke uses Matthew rather than Mark in the Triple Tradition (with Matthew having previously expanded upon Mark). On the 2DH the additional literary relationship comes about through Matthew's and Luke's independent use of Q (alongside Mark). The 2DH calls these passages "Mark–Q overlaps" because to explain the pattern of agreements the 2DH proposes that Mark and Q have parallel accounts of the same material. Supporters of the 2DH often suppose that in such cases Matthew combined Mark and Q, while Luke used Q alone.

We have encountered a number of these passages already. In the previous chapter we discussed the parable of the mustard seed (Mark 4:30–32 || Matt 13:31–32 || Luke 13:18–19) in the context of the "unpicking" objection. In the discussion of Luke's opening earlier in this chapter we came across additional major agreements in the teaching of John the Baptist and the temptation narrative. We have already argued that these parallels are best explained by Matthew adapting Mark and then Luke adapting Matthew. Other generally recognized major agreement passages include the Beelzebul controversy (Mark 3:22–30 || Matt 12:22–32 || Luke 11:14–23) and the mission charge (Mark 6:7–13 || Matt 10:1, 7–16 || Luke 9:1–6; 10:1–12). We can't look at all of these here, so we'll just examine the first of them, the Beelzebul controversy.

Luke's Knowledge of Matthew

Mark 3:22–30	Matt 12:22–32	Luke 11:14–23
	Then there was brought to him a blind and <u>dumb</u> demoniac. And he healed him, so that the <u>dumb man spoke</u> and saw. And all <u>the crowds were amazed</u> and were saying, "Can this be the son of David?"	And he was casting out a demon and it was <u>dumb</u>. And when the demon had come out <u>the dumb man was speaking</u> and <u>the crowds marvelled</u>.
And the scribes who came down from Jerusalem were saying, "He has Beelzebul" and "*By the ruler of the demons* he *casts out the demons.*" And summoning them he was saying *to them,* "How can Satan cast out Satan? And if *a kingdom is divided against itself,* that kingdom cannot stand. And if *a house is* divided against itself, that house will not be able to stand. *And if Satan* has risen up *against himself* and *is divided*, he cannot *stand* but has an end.	But when the Pharisees heard they said, "This man does not *cast out the demons* except *by* <u>Beelzebul</u> *the ruler of the demons.*" But knowing their <u>reflec-tions</u> he *said to them,* "<u>Every</u> *kingdom divided against itself* <u>is laid waste</u>, and every city or *house* divided against itself will not stand. *And if Satan* casts out Satan, he *is divided against himself*; <u>how</u>, then, <u>will his kingdom</u> *stand*?	But some of them said, "<u>By</u> <u>Beelzebul</u> *the ruler of the demons* he *casts out the demons,* but he, <u>knowing their thoughts,</u> <u>said</u> *to them,* "<u>Every</u> *king-dom divided against itself* <u>is laid waste</u> and *house* upon house falls. *And if Satan is divided against himself,* <u>how</u> <u>will his kingdom</u> *stand*? For you say by Beelzebul I cast out the demons.
	And <u>if I by Beelzebul cast out the demons, by whom do your sons cast out? On account of this they shall be your judges. But if by the spirit of God I cast out the demons, then has come upon you the kingdom of God.</u>	But <u>if I by Beelzebul cast out the demons, by whom do your sons cast out? On account of this they shall be your judges. But if by the finger of God I cast out the demons, then has come upon you the kingdom of God.</u>

Mark 3:22–30	Matt 12:22–32	Luke 11:14–23
But no one can enter into the house of *the strong man* and plunder his property unless first he binds the strong man, and then he will plunder his house.	Or how can one enter into the house of *the strong man* and plunder his property, unless first he binds the strong man? And then he will plunder his house.	When the fully armed *strong man* guards his own palace, his belongings are in peace. But when one stronger than he attacks and conquers him, he takes away his armor in which he trusted and distributes his spoils.
	Whoever is not with me is against me and whoever does not gather with me scatters.	Whoever is not with me is against me and whoever does not gather with me scatters.
Amen I say to you that everything will be forgiven the sons of men, the transgressions and whatever blasphemies they may blaspheme.	On account of this I say to you, every sin and blasphemy will be forgiven human beings, but blasphemy against the Spirit will not be forgiven.	
But whoever blasphemes *against the Holy Spirit* has no forgiveness but is guilty of an eternal sin." For they were saying, "He has an unclean spirit."	And whoever speaks a word against the Son of Man, it will be forgiven him, but whoever speaks *against the Holy Spirit* it will not be forgiven him, neither in this age nor in the one to come.	*Luke 12:10* And everyone who will speak a word against the Son of Man, it will be forgiven him; but the one who blasphemes *against the Holy Spirit* will not be forgiven.

The translation above is again over-literal so as to bring out the agreements and disagreements in the underlying Greek. Solid underlining indicates words that are common to Matthew and Luke but not Mark. Dashed underlining indicates near but not precise agreements between Matthew and Luke against Mark. Italics indicated wording that is identical, or nearly identical, in all three Gospels.

On the Farrer Hypothesis, Matthew's version can reasonably be regarded as a rhetorical elaboration of Mark's, designed to make Jesus' response to the charge against him (that he casts out demons by the power of Beelzebul) more effective by employing the kinds of techniques taught in ancient rhetorical handbooks. Matthew begins by supplying a particular occasion for the charge (the healing of a blind and dumb demoniac), changes the accusers from the contextually improbable Jerusalem-based scribes to the Pharisees, and clarifies the nature of the charge (Mark's potentially ambiguous "He has Beelzebul" might suggest either that Jesus controls Beelzebul or that he is possessed by Beelzebul). Matthew also clarifies Jesus' counter-arguments by tightening up the threefold structure (divided kingdom, divided house, divided Satan), and by moving "And if Satan casts out Satan" to the end of this trio so it both forms the conclusion of this section and becomes more clearly associated with Satan's division against himself. Matthew next strengthens Jesus' case by adding a further argument, effectively "If it were the case that I cast out demons by means of Satanic power, what would that say about your exorcists?" He then has Jesus affirm that far from showing that he is in league with the devil—which he has now shown to be absurd—his exorcisms are evidence of the imminence of God's kingdom. Matthew resumes his use of Mark by taking over the mini parable of the strong man virtually intact, as a graphic illustration that in order to cast out demons one must first neutralize their ruler. The insertion of the saying about gathering and scattering is presumably then intended as a warning to the Pharisees to consider whose side they are really on, a warning that is then reinforced by a clarified version of the sin against the Holy Spirit.

On this understanding, which has no need of Q to explain Matthew's additions and alterations to Mark, Luke composed his version on the basis of Matthew's (at a point in Luke's Gospel where we would expect him to be following Matthew rather than Mark, since, as we shall see in chapter 5, Luke's version of the Beelzebul controversy comes in its Matthean rather than its Markan sequence). Luke's indebtedness to Matthew is shown by the extent of the underlined text, not least in the saying about gathering and scattering, which otherwise has little obvious connection to its Lukan context (given that Luke relocates the Sin Against the Holy Spirit to a later point in his Gospel), and even more in the long string of words "if I by Beelzebul cast out demons . . . then has come upon you the kingdom of God."

This would constitute a string of 36 identical words in Greek apart from three minor differences: Luke's replacement of Matthew's καὶ εἰ (*kai de*—"and if") with εἰ δὲ (*ei de*—"but if"), the placement of ὑμων (*humōn*—"your") either before or after κριταὶ ἔσονται (*kritai esontai*—"will be your judges"), and Luke's "finger" in place of Matthew's "spirit."

Many scholars seem to take it as self-evident that the last of these differences is a change Luke would not have made, given his interest in the

Spirit, so that Luke could not have used Matthew here. But Luke is sparing in his reference to the Spirit between the fourth chapter of his Gospel and the start of Acts. Luke's change of "spirit of God" to "finger of God" is probably intended to create an allusion to Exod 8:19, where Pharaoh's magicians, unable to replicate the plague of gnats wrought through Aaron, declare "This is the finger of God" (the plague of gnats being the third of ten plagues God visits upon the Egyptians in order to persuade the Egyptian pharaoh, i.e., king, to let his people depart from Egypt). Luke thereby clarifies the distinction between Jesus' exorcisms and those of "your sons" (other Jewish exorcists): *their* exorcisms are akin to magic, while Jesus' herald the coming of God's kingdom (cf. the futile exorcistic antics of the sons of Sceva described at Acts 19:13–20, which result in a bonfire of magic books).

The Two Document Hypothesis regards the Beelzebul controversy as a Mark–Q overlap passage, in which Matthew has combined Mark and Q while Luke has largely followed Q alone. In addition to the argument we have just addressed over whether Luke could have changed "spirit" to "finger," advocates of the 2DH sometimes hold up this passage as a prime example of the unpicking objection we discussed in the previous chapter. According to this argument, Luke's use of Matthew looks problematic here since Luke appears to have taken over Matthew's additions to Mark more or less verbatim while rejecting what Matthew has most closely in common with Mark and adapting Matthew's adaptations of Mark still further, a procedure that suggests Luke would have been deliberately comparing Matthew with Mark in order to use only Matthew's additions and alterations to Mark (which would be a very odd and difficult thing to attempt).

The parallels do not bear this out, however. For one thing, the italicized text shows several places where Luke has preserved wording Matthew has taken over from Mark (so that despite what the 2DH objection claims, Luke does not systematically avoid Mark/Matthew agreements). For another, Luke's deviation from material Matthew shares closely with Mark occurs principally in Luke's reworking of the mini parable of the strong man from a domestic burglary to a military insurrection, which Luke may have thought fitted better with the images of a divided kingdom and a divided house (taking "house" in the sense of dynasty rather than household). Luke's version of the strong man parable looks quite Lukan in its wording, and is not especially characteristic of the hypothetical Q.

Overall, Luke is once again further removed from Mark than Matthew mainly because Matthew has reworked Mark and Luke has subsequently reworked Matthew, with Luke's further distance from Mark being the natural result.

The thesis that this set of parallels results from a Mark–Q overlap faces a number of difficulties:

1. If Q closely resembled Luke here, then Matthew will have needed to closely conflate two parallel sources, contrary to the normal practice of ancient authors who generally preferred to follow one source at a time for any single incident (we shall, however, have to qualify this point below).
2. If, on the other hand, Q more closely resembled Matthew, then Luke may as well be using Matthew as Q.
3. Moreover, if Q closely resembled Matthew where Matthew closely resembled Mark, then the close similarities between Mark and Q stand in need of explanation. Any direct dependence between Mark and Q would undermine the logic of the way in which Q is normally defined and reconstructed, which in turn could threaten the entire 2DH.
4. If Matthew and Luke were independently using Q here, it is quite a coincidence that they should both choose to copy Q quite so closely as they do in the two passages they independently add to Mark.
5. The saying about gathering and scattering fits loosely in its context here in Matthew and Luke and looks as if it could be an independent saying. It is too much of a coincidence that Matthew and Luke should have independently chosen to include it at precisely this point unless it stood at the corresponding point in Q. Yet it appears to be Matthew who connects this saying (with Διὰ τοῦτο—*dia touto*—"on account of this") with the saying about the sin against the Holy Spirit. Perhaps Matthew derived this entire sequence (strong man, gathering and scattering, sin against the Holy Spirit) from Q, but this poses a difficult dilemma for the 2DH. If Q's version of the sin against the Holy Spirit resembles Luke's (Luke 12:10) then Matthew has microconflated Mark and Q particularly closely, contrary to normal ancient working practices. If, however, Matthew more closely represents the text of Q here, then once again Luke's dependence on Q may as well be Luke's dependence on Matthew.

We have dealt with this example at some length to emphasize that, despite what proponents of the 2DH often claim, the major agreements support Luke's use of Matthew (along with Mark) far better than Matthew's and Luke's independent use of Mark and Q.

We should next take a quick look at the minor agreements. These are instances where Matthew and Luke agree against the text of Mark in the Triple Tradition (where all three Synoptic Gospels run roughly in parallel), but to a lesser extent than in the major agreements. It is hard to pin down a precise definition of what constitutes a minor agreement. They typically involve agreements of between one and five words in Matthew and Luke against Mark. Some scholars have also counted agreements in omission (where Matthew and Luke both omit the same material from a Markan passage), but it is unclear how and whether these should be counted. In what follows, we shall mostly restrict the term "minor agreement" to similar additions or changes that Matthew and Luke both make to Mark.

This is best explained by means of example, so we shall begin with one of the most striking, a cluster of minor agreements that occur in the account of Jesus' hearing before the high priest and Peter's denial (so which cannot conceivably be regarded as a Mark–Q overlap since Q is not meant to extend into the passion narrative).

Mark 14:72b, 65	Matthew 26:75, 67–68	Luke 22:61–64
And Peter remembered the word as Jesus said to him, "Before the cock crows twice you will deny me three times." And he broke down and was weeping.	And Peter remembered the word of Jesus which he had spoken, "Before the cock crows, you will deny me three times." And *he went outside and wept bitterly.*	And Peter remembered the word of the Lord as he said to him, "Before the cock crows today you will deny me three times." And *he went outside and wept bitterly.*
And some people began to spit at him [Jesus] and to cover his face and hit him and say to him, "Prophesy!" And the attendants received him with blows.	Then they spat into his [Jesus'] face and hit him and some slapped him, *saying,* "Prophesy to us, Anointed One, *who is it that struck you?"*	And the men who were holding him [Jesus] were mocking him, beating [him] and covering him they asked *saying,* "Prophesy, *who is that struck you?"*

Since Luke reorders Peter's denial in relation to Jesus' appearance before the Jewish high priest, we have had to present the Markan and Matthean versions out of order here to show how they parallel the text of Luke. We can then see three agreements of Luke and Matthew against Mark in these three verses of Luke.

One of these is very minor indeed, namely the common addition of "saying" (λέγοντες—*legontes*) to introduce the guards' mocking words. This is such a common way of introducing direct speech (given that the original text of the Gospels contained no quotation marks or other punctuation) that if this were the only minor agreement here it could reasonably be dismissed as purely coincidental.

The other two agreements are too extensive to be coincidental. The word for "bitterly" (πικρῶς—*pikrōs*) occurs nowhere else in the New Testament, so the odds against Matthew and Luke hitting upon it independently would seem to be astronomical, let alone those of their independently agreeing on the entire phrase ἐξελθὼν ἔξω ἔκλαυσεν πικρῶς (*exelthōn exō eklausen pikrōs*—"having gone away outside he wept bitterly") against Mark's ἐπιβαλὼν ἔκλαιεν (*epibalōn eklaien*—"having thrown [himself] down he was weeping"). The same applies to Matthew's and Luke's common addition of τίς ἐστιν ὁ παίσας σε (*tis estin ho paisas se*—"who is it that struck you?") after Mark's "prophesy." It is highly unlikely that these agreements could be the result of Matthew and Luke employing a common oral tradition (why would an *oral* tradition preserve just these words, and how much of a coincidence does it take for it to have reached Matthew and Luke in precisely the same form and for them to have independently inserted it into their own accounts?). The least implausible way to escape the otherwise inescapable conclusion that Luke must have known Matthew is to suggest that the text of one or other Gospel has been altered to conform to the other in the course of copying.

There is at least some potential evidence for this in the case of the "weeping bitterly" agreement, since a small number of manuscripts of Luke omit the verse in question (Luke 22:62), but there is no manuscript evidence to support the elimination of "who is it that struck you?" so here proponents of the Two Document Hypothesis have to appeal to conjectural emendation, that is to the supposition that the original text of one of the Gospels (in this case Matthew) has not survived in any extant manuscript but that one is nevertheless justified in emending the text we have to what one supposes it originally must have been. The conjectural emendation proposed here is supported by the claim that the addition of "who is it that struck you?" makes no sense in Matthew, since Matthew omits any mention of Jesus being blindfolded. But against this it may be suggested that Matthew envisages one group of guards spitting in Jesus' face while another group hit him from behind, or that Jesus is being asked to name someone previously unknown to him. In any case, neither the omission of Luke 22:62 nor that of "who is it that struck you" from Matthew commands the support of many text critics, and both appear in modern critical editions of the New Testament. The only real reason to excise both agreements is to save the Two Document Hypothesis. On the face of it, they point strongly to Luke's use of Matthew.

At this point, however, a defender of the 2DH might reasonably ask why Luke should incorporate such minor Matthean changes to Mark when he came to compose his own version. For Luke to carefully compare the Matthean and Markan versions of parallel passages to pick out and employ Matthean improvements would be hard to do given the format of ancient manuscripts and would thus be something an ancient author would be unlikely to attempt; as we've already said, ancient authors typically followed one source at a time without attempting to closely conflate two or more of them.

In the case of the minor agreements we've just looked at, we might plausibly suggest that at this point Luke is following Matthew rather than Mark (since there are more Luke/Matthew agreements against Mark than Luke/Mark agreements against Matthew in this section). This would then explain the minor agreements noted above. This explanation will not, however, work for passages where Luke appears to be following Mark in Mark's sequence and Matthew's sequence differs. One such example occurs in the healing of the paralytic:

Mark 2:1–12	Matthew 9:1–8	Luke 5:17–26
And entering again into Capernaum several days later it was heard that he was at home. And many people gathered so that there was no longer room [for them] nor at the door, and he was speaking the word to them.	And after boarding a boat he crossed over and came to his own city.	And it came to pass on one of the days when he was teaching and there were Pharisees and teachers of the law sitting who had come from every town of Galilee and Judea and Jerusalem; and the power of the Lord to heal was in him.

Luke's Knowledge of Matthew

Mark 2:1-12	Matthew 9:1-8	Luke 5:17-26
And they came carrying to him a paralytic *borne by four people*.	And *behold* they brought to him a paralytic placed *on a bed*.	And *behold* men carrying *on a bed* a man who was paralyzed
And not being able to approach him on account of the crowd they unroofed the roof where he was, and after digging through, they let down the pallet on which the paralytic was lying.		and they were seeking to bring him in and to put him before him. And not finding by what way to bring him in on account of the crowd they went up onto the roof and let him down through the tiles with the mini-bed into the midst in front of Jesus.
And when Jesus saw their faith he says to the paralytic, "Child, your sins are forgiven." But some of the scribes were sitting there and pondering in their hearts, "Why does this man speak thus? He is blaspheming! Who can forgive sins except one – God?" And immediately, Jesus, recognizing *in his spirit* that they were pondering thus within themselves says to them, "Why do you ponder these things in your hearts? Which is easier, to say *to the paralytic*, 'Your sins are forgiven' or to say, 'Get up *and pick up your pallet* and walk'? But in order that you may know that the Son of Man has authority to forgive sins on earth—" He says to the paralytic, "I say to you, get up, pick up your pallet and depart to your house."	And when Jesus saw their faith he *said* to the paralytic, "Take heart, child, your sins are forgiven." *And* behold, some of the scribes said in themselves, "This man is "blaspheming!" And seeing *their* thoughts, Jesus *said*, "For what reason are you thinking evil things in your hearts? For which is easier, to say, 'Your sins are forgiven' or to say, 'Get up and walk'? But in order that you may know that the Son of Man has authority →*on earth* to forgive sins –" Then he says to the paralytic, "After getting up, pick up your <u>bed</u> and depart to your house."	And when he saw their faith, he *said*, "Man, your sins have been forgiven you." *And* the scribes and the Pharisees began to ponder, saying, "Who is this man who speaks blasphemies? Who can forgive sins except God alone?" But recognizing *their* ponderings, he *said* to them in reply, "Why do you ponder in your hearts? Which is easier, to say, 'Your sins have been forgiven' or to say, Get up and walk?' But in order that you may know that the Son of Man has authority →*on earth* to forgive sins—" he said to the paralytic, "I say to you, get up and pick up your mini-<u>bed</u> and go to your house."

Mark 2:1-12	Matthew 9:1-8	Luke 5:17-26
And he got up and after immediately picking up the pallet he went out in front of them all, so that they were all astonished and glorified God, saying, "We have never seen anything like it!"	And after getting up, he *went away to his house*. Now when the crowds saw they were *afraid* and glorified God, who gave such authority to human beings.	And having at once got up in their presence, he picked up what he had been lying on and *went away to his house* glorifying God. And amazement took them all and they were glorifying God and they were filled with *fear*, saying, "We have seen remarkably unexpected things today!"

There are various kinds of Matthew/Luke agreement here, which have been marked in different ways in the table above. Italics in the Matthew and Luke columns indicates words shared by Matthew and Luke that differ from Mark, whereas italics in the Mark column indicate words that Matthew and Luke agree in omitting from identical Markan contexts. An arrow (→) before an italicized phrase indicates where Matthew and Luke agree in changing the order of Mark's words.

Many of these agreements appear individually trivial. Changing the historic present "says" to "said" (λέγει—*legei* to εἶπεν—*eipen*) is an improvement that could easily occur to two writers independently. Similarly, two writers might independently hit on adding the word "behold" (ἰδού—*idou*) at the same point in the narrative to alert the reader to an interesting development. Moving the words "on earth" immediately after "has authority" is again an improvement that two writers might readily make independently. That the onlookers should react with fear (or awe) is hardly an uncommon trope in the Gospels and is differently expressed in Matthew and Luke.

Whether two writers would independently choose to omit precisely the same words ("to the paralytic" and "and pick up your pallet") from precisely the same context is less clear. One could make a case that two writers seeking to abbreviate their source might independently find these phrases redundant and so omit them, but it does seem something of a coincidence. The change from "pallet" (κράβαττον—*krabatton*) to "bed" (κλίνη—*klinē*) is an even less obvious change to make, not least since one would imagine a bed would be a less suitable thing to carry someone around on than a pallet, which may be why Luke elsewhere uses the diminutive form κλινίδιον (*klinidion*—here awkwardly translated "mini-bed" in order to indicate its relation to the word for "bed"). It is also striking that Luke and Matthew both insert the phrase ἐπὶ κλίνης (*epi klinēs*—"on a bed") into a context in which Mark mentions neither bed nor pallet. Even more striking is Matthew's and Luke's agreeing on replacing Mark's "went out in front of them all" with "went away to his house" (ἀπῆλθεν εἰς τὸν οἶκον αὐτοῦ—*apēlthen eis ton oikon autou*). It could perhaps be argued that here Matthew and Luke independently picked up on the wording of the command Jesus had just given the paralytic, which occurs in the previous verse in Mark, but if so then they would have coincidentally also agreed in changing Mark's word for "go away" (ὕπαγε—*hupage*) to the different verb ἀπῆλθεν (*apēlthen*).

Whatever one makes of these minor Matthew/Luke agreements individually, their cumulative significance cannot be lightly dismissed. So many agreements clustered together in one passage seem far less likely to arise from coincidence than is any of the agreements taken in isolation. In combination they strongly suggest that Luke's adaptation of Mark must have been influenced by Matthew.

But this leads us straight back to the problem mentioned above: why would Luke be influenced by Matthew here? From Luke 4:31 to 6:19, Luke is following Mark in Mark's order (from Mark 1:21 to 3:19, with a slight re-ordering towards the end of this section). Matthew, however, has radically re-ordered this section of Mark so that much of it falls into his collection of miracle and controversy stories in Matthew 8 and 9, following the Sermon on the Mount (Matt 5–7), which Luke parallels at Luke 6:17–49. So why on earth would Luke scroll forward through Matthew to pick up a few minor changes from Matthew's much abbreviated version of the healing of the paralytic when he has just reached Mark's fuller account, which he takes as the basis of his own? If ever there was a place where one would expect Luke to follow the common ancient practice of using one source at a time, this is surely it.

And yet the implausibility of Luke's apparent procedure hardly does away with the improbability of the coincidences if he was not influenced by Matthew. The most likely scenario, then, is that Luke was primarily working from memory of both his sources. He may have refreshed his memory of Mark by reading through a section of it (probably more than one passage) before composing his own version of the corresponding section for his own Gospel, but he probably didn't have eye contact with any written source when he actually came to compose (either by writing or, more likely, via dictation). His memory of Mark's version was then contaminated by his memory of Matthew's (which is not improbable if he knew both reasonably well), with the result that he ended up taking over several of Matthew's changes to Mark. While we can't be certain that this is what happened, it is hard to see how else to explain the Luke/Matthew agreements we find here. (At this point the astute reader may realize the need to qualify the argument concerning the difficulty of Matthew conflating Mark and Q, since in principle this could be similarly explained by Matthew's relying on his memory of both texts; this does not, however, negate anything else that was said about this major agreement.)

Minor agreements extend well beyond the examples we have just given. They occur throughout the Triple Tradition, albeit with varying frequency. Estimates of the total number of these agreements vary from about seven hundred to around three thousand. The discrepancy in these counts arises from the lack of any consensus on what counts as a minor agreement and thus how they should be enumerated. As we have just seen when looking at the Healing of the Paralytic, there are different types of minor agreement between Matthew and Luke. Aggregating them together into a single total may thus be a little like trying to aggregate a count of apples, tomatoes, peas, and pebbles. In any case the raw number of agreements comes nowhere close to telling the full story, since what matters isn't just the quantity of agreements but their quality. An agreement of a rare word such as "bitterly" counts for far more than that of a common word such as "and." Agreement of a string of words (or a complete phrase) is more significant than agreements between each of the individual words taken in isolation. Many people would regard the common addition of words as more significant than the common omission of words. A reordering of words or expressing a similar thought in different words may or may not count as a significant agreement. A cluster of agreements within a single passage surely carries more weight than does any of the agreements considered in isolation; in such cases the whole is surely more than the sum of its parts. The significance of minor agreements cannot be ascertained by statistics alone. What we can say is that there are quite enough high-quality and/or clustered minor agreements of Matthew and Luke against Mark to render the supposition of their independent use of Mark highly problematic.

Many advocates of the Two Document Hypothesis recognize that the minor agreements pose a problem for the 2DH, but then generally respond with one or more of the following counterarguments:

1. It may be argued that once the multitude of trivial agreements (such as adding "and" or changing an historic present to a past) are discounted, the number of agreements that is left is not nearly so impressive. But

this ignores both the quality of those that remain and the significance of agreements occurring in clusters.

2. It is sometimes suggested that the minor agreements are due to Luke and Matthew having used either an earlier or later edition of Mark (Proto-Mark or Deutero-Mark) than that now available to us. But while it is likely that the manuscripts of Mark available to Matthew and Luke were not identical to any modern critical text of Mark, there is no evidence for the existence of either a Proto-Mark or a Deutero-Mark capable of explaining the minor agreements. The only reason for postulating the existence of this different edition of Mark is to save the Two Document Hypothesis.

3. It is more plausibly suggested that while many of the minor agreements may be purely coincidental (being, for example, obvious improvements that might occur to two authors working independently), the remainder are due to textual variants. No two manuscript copies of the Gospels were identical, and in the course of copying we might expect the text of each Gospel to contaminate that of the others. Copyists might well assimilate the text of a less familiar Gospel (Luke, say) to that of one they were more familiar with (Matthew, say), thereby giving rise to the appearance of many minor agreements, which were not, however, present in the original texts of Matthew and Luke. But while (as we have seen) there is some manuscript evidence that some minor agreements might be explained in this way, there are many other minor agreements for which there is little or no manuscript evidence to suggest they arose through textual assimilation. While it might be reasonable to conjecture the existence of an earlier text type supported by no manuscript evidence to explain a handful of minor agreements if that were all there were, to do so to explain away all the minor agreements we in fact find is to bend the evidence to fit the theory. Moreover, textual assimilation might be expected to eliminate as many minor agreements as it created (if the process of copying manuscripts caused a tendency for the texts of Matthew and Luke to become assimilated to each other, then it should also cause a similar tendency for the texts of Matthew and Mark and of Luke and Mark, which would tend to eliminate agreements against Mark). Finally, any mutual assimilation of the texts of the three Synoptic Gospels can only have been partial at best, since we are still left with three quite distinct Gospels, often with quite distinct wording in parallel passages.

4. It is occasionally suggested that those minor agreements that can't otherwise be explained away are due to Matthew's and Luke's use of some other common source besides Mark. Sometimes the proposed source is Q, thereby expanding the list of Mark–Q overlap passages. But apart from the fact that Q is then in some danger of growing to resemble Matthew or Luke, this cannot account for any agreements in the infancy and passion narratives, which Q is not meant to have. It may also strike many people as a measure of desperation to appeal to a Mark–Q overlap to explain relatively minor agreements; do they appear so minor because the text of Q is so similar to that of Mark in these passages? If so, how are such similarities between Mark and Q to be explained? Much the same objection would apply to the appeal to any additional written source, together with the charge that this would involve multiplying hypothetical sources in an uncontrolled way just to save the 2DH. Appeal to a common oral tradition behind Matthew and Luke fares no better, since it is hard to see how an oral tradition could give rise to such precise agreements of written texts against their principal written source, except perhaps in very rare cases where it could be argued that the putative oral tradition preserved a particular apt or poetic phrasing that might stick in memory. In the main, though, the appeal to oral tradition relies rather too much on the vagueness with which it is invoked to have any real plausibility.

To the extent that all these arguments against the significance of the minor agreements fail to convince, the minor agreements remain problematic for the Two Document Hypothesis and supportive of the Farrer Hypothesis.

There is one other kind of Matthew/Luke agreement we may mention briefly here, and that is the surprising extent of verbatim agreement in parts of the Double Tradition (that is, the virtually exact verbal agreement in some passages that the 2DH regards as having been taken from Q). This is by no means evident throughout the Double Tradition. Some DT parallels, such as the parable of the talents in Matthew (Matt 25:14–30) and the parable of the pounds in Luke (Luke 19:11–27), have scarcely a word in common. But there are several others where Matthew and Luke are virtually word-for-word the same.

We have met several of these already in the preaching of John the Baptist and the principal addition to the Beelzebul controversy. Other examples include the saying about the difficulty of serving two masters

(Matt 6:24 || Luke 16:13), the return of the unclean spirit (Matt 12:43-45 || Luke 11:24-26), and the woe on Galilean cities (Matt 11:21-23a || Luke 10:13-15). Equally striking are substantial strings of words that are identical in Matthew and Luke, the longest in the Double Tradition extending to 27 words at Matt 11:25b-27 || Luke 10:21b-22, with strings of 25 and 24 identical words respectively occurring at Matt 8:9-10 || Luke 7:8-9 and Matt 12:41 || Luke 11:32. At first sight this may seem easy enough for the 2DH to explain: these and others like them are passages that Matthew and Luke will both have copied from Q. But for this explanation to work, Matthew and Luke must time and again have independently decided to copy Q verbatim at precisely the same points. This would be quite a coincidence.

As already mentioned, the degree of verbal agreement between Matthew and Luke across DT parallels varies from almost total to virtually none, so it's not as if Matthew and Luke have a consistent policy of copying this material exactly. It's thus strange that Matthew and Luke should hit on the same passages to copy closely from Q if they are working independently, especially since this happens much less often in their use of Mark. One might argue that the Double Tradition contains a much higher proportion of words spoken by Jesus and John the Baptist than does Mark, and that Matthew and Luke might both be disposed to preserve the wording of such material more closely. But even if we restrict ourselves to the sayings material in each case, Matthew and Luke still tend to correspond to each other more closely in the Double Tradition (when on the 2DH they'd be using Q) than in the Triple Tradition (where they'd be using Mark).

The problem is much diminished, however, if we suppose that rather than Matthew and Luke making independent use of Q (alongside Mark), Luke is directly using Matthew (alongside Mark). Just as Luke chooses to rewrite some Markan passages more thoroughly than others, so he varies his treatment of the material he takes from Matthew. Passages where high verbatim agreement occurs between Matthew and Luke then arise where Luke has chosen to keep Matthew's wording virtually intact. This explanation does not need to appeal to the coincidence of Luke and Matthew independently choosing to do the same with Q.

Conclusion

The Two Document Hypothesis argues that Luke cannot have known and used Matthew; the Farrer Hypothesis argues that he did. In this chapter we have reviewed various similarities between Matthew and Luke that suggest a direct dependence between the two. Luke's opening resembles Matthew's opening in a number of ways, and even where their infancy narratives appear to differ substantially, this can be seen as arising from Luke imitating Matthew in much the same way as he imitates the opening of 1 Samuel (along with other OT passages). We have also seen how Matthew's apparent influence on Luke extends beyond the infancy narratives well into the respective fourth chapters of these two Gospels and is arguably present in their resurrection accounts as well. A brief survey of the major and minor agreements between Matthew and Luke indicates numerous places throughout both Gospels where the similarities between Matthew and Luke are easier to explain if Luke used Matthew than if the two Evangelists made independent use of Mark and Q. Finally, the high degree of verbal agreement between Matthew and Luke in quite a few Double Tradition parallels is easier to explain if Luke was using Matthew directly than if Matthew and Luke were making independent use of Q.

These arguments are overlapping, but they are also mutually reinforcing. While each of them individually points to Luke's use of Matthew, taken together they make Luke's use of Matthew hard to resist. It is not just that the Farrer Hypothesis can counter the common arguments *against* Luke's use of Matthew (as we saw in the previous chapter); the Farrer Hypothesis can also make a strong case that Luke *must* have used Matthew.

But there is one large piece of the Synoptic Puzzle we have yet to examine: the question of order. Does the order of the Double Tradition material in Matthew and Luke undermine the plausibility of Luke's use of Matthew, as the 2DH argues, or might it turn out to support it further? We shall tackle this question in the next chapter.

5

An Orderly Account?

Comparing Orders

AT A SUFFICIENT LEVEL of generality, Matthew and Luke follow quite similar orders. They both begin with accounts of Jesus' conception and birth, followed by the preaching of John the Baptist, Jesus' baptism and temptation, an account of the various things Jesus said and did in the course of his ministry (often in much the same sequence in both Gospels), and conclude with the accounts of his last few days in Jerusalem, the Last Supper, Jesus' arrest, trial, and crucifixion, the empty tomb, and resurrection appearances. But, as ever, the devil lurks in the detail, not least the detailed sequence of events between Jesus' baptism and passion. Where Jesus' ministry follows a similar sequence in Luke and Matthew, this is usually because both Gospels are following Mark. Where one or the other Gospel either diverges from Mark's order or uses non-Markan material, their agreement in order usually disappears.

This can be seen more clearly from Table 5.1 below, which sets out the parallels between Luke, Matthew, and Mark in Luke's order, thereby showing both the extent to which FH Luke followed the order of material in his sources and the extent to which he departed from it. Column A shows Matthean parallels in Matthew's sequence, column B Matthean parallels that depart from Matthew's sequence, column C Markan parallels in Mark's sequence, and Column D Markan parallels out of Mark's sequence. Italics in the Luke column denote special L material, that is Lukan material for which there is no (clear) Markan or Matthean parallel. Italics in the other four columns denotes passages which FH Luke has substantially adapted (by imitation or other substantial rewriting) from the parallel proposed. These are mainly adaptations discussed in the previous chapter.

The table has been simplified to make it easier to follow. In particular, it does not indicate internal rearrangement within blocks of material, for example at Luke 11:24–32 || Matt 12:22–45; Luke 11:37–54 || Matt 23:6–36; and Luke 17:20–37 || Matt 24:23–41. In these blocks FH Luke has taken over all, some, or most of the material from the corresponding Matthean block but rearranged it into a different order, occasionally combining it with small amounts of his own material or material taken from elsewhere.

Luke	Matthew		Mark	
	A	B	C	D
1–2	1–2			
3:1—4:13	3:1—4:11		(1:2–13)	
4:14–30	4:12–16			6:1–6a
4:31–44			1:21–39	
5:1–11				4:1–2; 1:16–20
5:10—6:19			1:40—3:19	
6:20—7:10	5, 7, 8:5–10	10:25–25a; 12:33–35		
7:11–17				
7:18–35	11:2–19			
7:36–50				14:3–9
8:1–3				
8:4–18			4:1–25	
8:19–21				3:31–35
8:22–56			4:35—5:43	
9:1–9			6:6b–16	
9:10–17			6:30–44	
9:18–50			8:27—9:10, 9:12–41	
9:51–56				
9:57–62	8:19–22			
10:1–12	9:37–38; 10:7–15			
10:13–15	11:20–24			
10:16		10:40		
10:17–20				
10:21–24	11:25–27	13:16–17		
10:25–28			12:28–34	

An Orderly Account?

Luke	Matthew		Mark	
	A	B	C	D
10:29-42				
11:1-4		6:9-13		
11:5-8				
11:9-13		7:7-11		
11:14-32	12:22-45			
11:33				4:21
11:34-36		6:22-23		
11:37-54		23:6-36		7:1, 5
12:1		15:6?		8:15?
12:2-9		10:26-33		
12:10	12:32			
12:13-21				
12:22-34		6:25-34, 19-21		
12:35-48		25:8-12; 24:43-51		
12:49-53		10:34-36		
12:54-56		16:2-3		
12:57-59		5:25-26		
13:1-17				
13:18-21	13:31-33			
12:22-30		7:13-23; 8:11-12		
13:31-33				
13:34-35		23:37-39		
14:1-14				
14:15-24		22:1-14		
14:25-33		10:37-38		
14:34-35		5:13		
15:1-7	18:12-14			
15:8—16:12				
16:13		6:24		
16:14-15				
16:16-17		11:12-13; 5:18		
16:18		19:9; 5:32		
16:19-31				
17:1-4	18:6-7, 15, 21-2			
17:5-6		17:19-21		
17:7-19				
17:20-37	24:23-41	10:39		

Solving the Synoptic Puzzle

Luke	Matthew		Mark	
	A	B	C	D
18:1–14		(23:12)		
18:15–43			10:13–34, 46–52	
19:1–10				
19:11–27	25:14–30			
19:28–40			11:1–10	
19:41–44				
19:45–48			11:15–19	
20:1–40			11:27—12:27	
20:41—21:36			12:35—13:37	
21:37–38				
22:1–23			14:1–2, 10–25	
22:24–30		20:24–28; 19:28		10:41–45
22:31–34			14:29–31	
22:35–38				
22:39–53			14:32–52	
22:54–71	26:54–75		(14:53–72)	
23:1–3			15:1–2	
23:4–16				
23:17–26			15:6–14, 20b–21	
23:27–31				
23:32–39			15:22–32	
23:40–43				
23:44–56			15:33–47	
24:1–12	(28:1–10, 17)		16:1–8	
24:13–35				
24:36–53	28:16–20			

Table 5.1 FH Luke's Use of Matthew and Mark

This outline is skeletal, but it enables us to make some initial observations:

1. Column A shows Luke and Matthew following a common order for much of their shared material from the start to the end of both Gospels. The 2DH can explain this as mostly due to their both following the order of Q—this is, after all, part of the 2DH case for seeing Q as a single document—but it is also compatible with Luke employing Matthew and Mark in alternating blocks and working steadily forwards through both. While FH Luke does frequently diverge from Matthew's

order, column A shows FH Luke's absolute position in Matthew as he works forwards through both his main sources.

2. Most of Luke's divergences from Matthew's order occur between Luke 10:16 and 17:6, which is roughly co-extensive with Luke's long central section, otherwise known as his travel narrative.

3. Prior to Luke 10:16, Luke diverges from Matthew's order no more than he does from Mark's. The main item he takes out of Matthew's order prior to Luke 10:16 concerns Jesus' response to a question John sends from prison (Luke 7:18–35 || Matt 11:2–19). This clearly has to come before Luke 9:7–9, which presupposes John the Baptist's death. If FH Luke wanted to use this material, he had no option but to bring it forward from its Matthean sequence.

4. Most of the material in Column B (Matthean material out of Matthew's order) concerns sayings of Jesus, which are more readily reordered into new topical sequences than narrative material (which Luke mainly takes over from Mark). As noted above, most of this material appears in Luke's central section, which is where (on any theory of Synoptic relationships) Luke has chosen to concentrate the bulk of Jesus' teaching. For the most part this reordered Matthean material is not relocated from one Markan context into a different one, but rather from a Matthean context (such as the Sermon on the Mount or the mission discourse) into a fresh context devised by Luke.

5. Since the order of Q is thought to be largely reflected in the order of Luke, column B indicates not only FH Luke's reordering of Matthean material, but also 2DH Matthew's reordering of Q. This can be seen by imagining what would happen to the Lukan parallels (and hence the order of the Q parallels) if they were reordered to bring column B into Matthew's order.

6. In one or two places where Mark and Matthew run closely in parallel, it is not always obvious which of them FH Luke will have followed. This is why parallel passages from both Mark and Matthew occasionally occur in the table above, with the arguably less likely option in parentheses. In particular, the text of Luke 22:54–71 (the account of Jesus' hearing before the high priest and Peter's denial) looks closer to that of Matt 26:54–75 than to that of Mark 14:53–72, so the table suggests that FH Luke chose to follow Matthew rather than Mark at this point.

7. Column A contains several substantial gaps in the sequence of Matthean material. Some of these are due to Luke's use of Matthean material out of Matthew's sequence, but the bulk of the gaps occur where either (a) Matthew contains material shared with Mark that Luke uses elsewhere, in its Markan sequence (e.g., Matt 8–9, 14:13–21; 16:13—17:8; 19:13–30; 20:17–19, 29–34, plus the bulk of the Jerusalem narrative in Matt 21–23, 26–27) or (b) Matthean material FH Luke doesn't use at all, including material shared by Matthew and Mark but not Luke (e.g., Matt 14:1–12; 14:22—16:10; 17:9–13; 19:3–12). Column A thus accounts for more of the common order of the material Luke shares with Matthew than the gaps in the Matthean sequence might at first make it appear.

These observations constitute only the first step in the argument, by clearing away some potential misunderstandings, showing at least some degree of common order, and highlighting where the main problems remain (largely in Luke's central section). The second step in the argument will build on point 7 above.

Hidden Parallels

We have suggested that Luke uses Matthew at the beginning and end of his Gospel, not through a straightforward copy-and-edit technique (i.e., copying or closely paraphrasing Matthew's text), but through more radical transformations that borrow elements of Matthew's material and work them into a fresh composition, resulting in a (more or less close) imitation of Matthew (sometimes in conjunction with other sources such as Mark or the Old Testament). This raises the question whether Luke might sometimes do something similar with other parts of Matthew to which he does not have direct and obvious parallels.

After Luke 4:30, FH Luke follows Mark until he switches back to Matthew at Luke 6:20 for the Sermon on the Plain, a radically abbreviated parallel to Matthew's Sermon on the Mount (to which we shall return below). He continues to follow Matthew beyond the Sermon to the story about the Capernaum centurion (Luke 7:1–10 || Matt 8:5–13), passing over the healing of the Leper at Matt 8:1–4, which he has already used at Luke 5:12–15 (in parallel with Mark 1:40–45). By usual reckoning, Luke 7:11—8:3 then constitutes a block of L material (material unique to Luke) surrounding the Double Tradition (on the FH, Matthean) block of John the Baptist material at Luke 7:18–35 ‖ Matt 11:2–19. Conversely, the bulk of Matt 8–9 consists mainly of Markan miracle and controversy stories that Matthew has deployed out of their Markan order and which Luke largely parallels elsewhere. There are, however, some indications that some material in Matt 8–9 influenced some of the L material in Luke 7:11—8:3.

The report of Jesus' preaching tour at Luke 8:1–2a resembles that at Matt 9:35; both mention towns and villages, and Jesus healing and preaching the good news of the kingdom. The L story of the raising of the widow's son at Nain at Luke 7:11–17 looks like an imitation of the resuscitation performed by Elijah (1 Kgs 17:17–24) but may in part have also been prompted by the raising of the ruler's daughter at Matt 9:18–19, 23–26, with both stories preparing for the statement that "the dead are raised" at Luke 7:22 ‖ Matt 11:5. Notably, the two raising stories both end with similar notices (absent from the parallel at Mark 5:35–43) that Jesus' action resulted in the spread of his fame over a wide area (Luke 7:17 ‖ Matt 9:26). The L story of the sinful woman who washes Jesus' feet at Luke 7:36–50 is Luke's nearest equivalent to Mark's anointing story at Mark 14:3–9, but it shares with Matt 9:2 an announcement of the forgiveness of sins (Luke 7:48b = Matt 9:2b, Ἀφέωνταί σου αἱ ἁμαρτίαι—*Apheōntai sou hai hamartia*—"your sins are forgiven"), with Matt 9:10–11 a Pharisaic complaint about Jesus consorting with sinners in the context of a meal, and with Matt 9:20–22 a woman who touches Jesus from behind (Luke 7:38; Matt 9:20) and is subsequently told that her faith has saved her (Luke 7:50b = Matt 9:22b:Ἡ πίστις σου σέσωκέν σε—*Hē pistis sou sesōken se*—"Your faith has saved/healed you"). Matthew's influence on Luke here thus looks similar in kind, if not in extent, to that we have suggested in Luke 1–4. We may term this kind of oblique influence a *hidden parallel*, meaning a passage in Luke that has been influenced by Matthew without being a straightforward copy or paraphrase.

Luke's central section contains quite a few hidden parallels with Matthew, which like those discussed above, occur in pretty much the same sequence in both Gospels. We shall leave until later the question how and why Luke may have worked in this way, but for now we may start by listing the twelve most salient hidden parallels that may be suggested for Luke's central section, along with a brief explanation of each:

1. *Matt 10:5 → Luke 9:52–56*: Where Matthew has Jesus tell the disciples not to enter any Samaritan town, Luke has Jesus' disciple enter a Samaritan town that rejects them.

2. *Matt 12:1–7 → Luke 10:25–37*: The Matthean passage is the parallel to the Markan story about Jesus' disciples plucking corn on the Sabbath, to which Matthew adds a couple of points of his own. One of these is Jesus' question about reading in the Law (Matt 12:5), which is similar to the question Jesus asks the scribe at Luke 10:26, while the parable of the good Samaritan that follows could be taken as an illustration of the quotation from Hos 6:6 that Matthew adds at Matt 12:7: "I desire mercy and not sacrifice" (cf. Luke 10:37). (It's possible that the love command also prompted recall of Matt 5:43–48, another passage that the parable of the good Samaritan would neatly illustrate, given the proverbial hostility between Jews and Samaritans).

3. *Matt 12:33–37 → Luke 11:39–52*: The direct Matthean parallel to this set of Lukan woes against the Pharisees and scribes comes at Matt 23:4–36, but its relocation to this point in Luke may have been prompted by the harsh words Jesus directs against the Pharisees at Matt 12:33–37; both Matt 12:33–35 and Luke 11:39–40 contrast outward show with inner depravity.

4. *Matt 13:1–50 → Luke 12:16—13:30*: Matthew's parable discourse contains themes and images that are also found in this section of Luke, such as an abundant harvest (Matt 13:8), gathering the harvest into barns (Matt 13:30), and the danger of riches (Matt 13:22), which all feature in Luke's parable of the rich fool (Luke 12:16–20), the burning of grass or weeds (Luke 12:28; Matt 13:30), the prospect of eschatological judgment (Luke 12:35—13:9, 13:22–30; Matt 13:30, 36–42), and a saying about weeping and gnashing teeth (Luke 13:28; Matt 13:50), which Luke admittedly draws from Matt 8:11–12, but this could have been cued by Matt 13:50.

5. *Matt 14:1–13 → Luke 13:31–33*: Both passages concern Herod in connection with the threatened or actual death of a prophet together with Jesus' actual or recommended withdrawal.

6. *Matt 14:1–21 → Luke 14:7–24*: In Matthew, Jesus and Herod host very different meals; Herod's banquet and Jesus' feeding of the crowds reflect the different kinds of guests Jesus speaks about (Luke 14:12–14) in between a pair of parables about feasts and banquets (Luke 14:7–11, 15–24).

7. *Matt 16:24–26 → Luke 14:25–27*: The direct Matthean parallel here occurs at Matt 10:37–38, but if Luke is working forward through

Matthew, the theme of cross-bearing discipleship could have been suggested by Matt 16:24-26.

8. *Matt 18:23-34 → Luke 16:1-12*: Matthew's parable of the two debtors and Luke's parable of the dishonest steward both concern servants who are worried about settling accounts with their masters. In Luke, the dishonest steward forgives part of the debts owed to his master; in Matthew's parable the lord forgives his slave's debt.

9. *Matt 19:1-26 → Luke 16:16-31*: Luke's train of thought is notoriously hard to follow at this point, but here Luke and Matthew both move from teaching on divorce to a story about the danger of riches.

10. *Matt 21:21 → Luke 17:6*: The saying about faith at Luke 17:6 is closest to Matt 17:19-20, but also resembles Matt 21:21. While Matt 21:21 speaks of faith moving mountains into the sea, it does so in the context of Jesus just having caused a fig tree (τῆς συκῆς—*tēs sukēs*) to wither, which taken together may well be the source of Luke's odd saying about faith transporting a sycamine tree (τῇ συκαμίνῳ ταύτῃ—*tē sukaminō tautē*) into the sea.

11. *Matt 20:29-33 → Luke 17:11-19*. Both stories concerned people (in Matthew two blind men, in Luke ten lepers) whom Jesus heals towards the end of his journey to Jerusalem, and who address Jesus in similar terms: ἔκραξαν λέγοντες· ἐλέησον ἡμᾶς, κύριε (*ekraxen legontes: eleēson hēmas—kyrie*—"they cried out saying, 'have mercy on us, Lord'"; Matt 20:30, 31); αὐτοὶ ἦραν φωνὴν λέγοντες· Ἰησοῦ ἐπιστάτα, ἐλέησον ἡμᾶς (*autoi ēran phōnēn legontes, Iēsou epistata, eleēson hēmas*—"they raised their voice saying, 'Jesus, master, have mercy on us'"; Luke 17:13).

12. *Matt 24:29-31, 44-51 → Luke 18:1-8*. Luke's parable of the importunate widow is ostensibly about prayer, but its conclusion concerns the vindication of the elect and the coming of the Son of Man (Luke 18:7-8). Similar themes are found at Matt 24:30-31 (which speaks of the coming of the Son of Man followed by the gathering of the elect). The word "elect" (ἐκλεκτός—*eklektos*) occurs only here in Luke, but three times in Mark and the parallel passages in Matthew (including Matt 24:31). Moreover, both Luke 18:8 and Matt 24:44-51 are concerned with whether the Son of Man will find faithful service at his coming.

If these twelve hidden parallels are inserted into the Matthean sequence shown in Column A in Table 5.1 for Luke 6:20—19:27, the following sequence of Luke–Matthew parallels results (with the hidden parallels shown in italics in the Matthew column of Table 5.2):

Luke	Matthew
6:20–7:10	5, 7, 8:5–10
7:11–17	*9:18-19, 23-26*
7:18–35	
7:36–50	*9:2b, 10-11, 22b*
8:1–3	*9:35*
8:4–9:50	[Mark 3:31–9:41]
9:51-56	*10:5*
9:57–62	8:19–22
10:1–12	9:37–38; 10:7–15
10:13–15	11:20–24
10:16–20	
10:21–24	11:25–27
10:25–37	*12:1-7*
11:1–32	
11:14–32	12:22–45
11:33–36	
11:39–52	*12:33-37*
12:1–9	
12:10	12:32
12:11–15	
12:16–13:30	*13:1-50*
13:18–21	13:31–33
13:31–33	*14:1-13*
14:1–6	
14:7–24	*14:1-21*
14:25–27	16:24–26
14:28–35	
15:1–7	18:12–14
15:8–32	
16:1–12	*18:23-34*
16:13–15	
16:16–31	*19:1-26*

An Orderly Account?

Luke	Matthew
16:18	
16:19-31	
17:1-4	18:6-7, 15, 21-2
17:5-10	
17:6	21:21
17:7-10	
17:11-19	20:29-33
17:20-37	24:23-41
18:1-8	24:29-31, 44-51
18:9-19:10	
19:11-27	25:14-30

Table 5.2—Clear and Hidden Parallels

While the Matthean sequence here isn't perfect, it comes close to exhibiting a consistently forward movement through Matthew. The slight deviations from Matthew's order can plausibly be explained by (a) Luke's need to arrange his material in a way that makes sense on its own terms and (b) Luke's working through Matthew block by block, where a block may be a fairly substantial body of material and not simply a single verse, paragraph, or pericope (a self-contained unit such as complete parable). That is, we should envisage Luke reading (or recalling) a substantial block of Matthew before composing his own corresponding block, and sometimes rearranging Matthean material within that block to suit his own design.

These hidden parallels cannot be explained by appeal to Q. For the most part the italicized Matthean passages in Table 5.2 occur either in material normally regarded as unique to Matthew or in material Matthew has taken from Mark. Occasionally (as in Matt 12:1-7 → Luke 10:25-37) the hidden parallel relies on Matthew's redaction of Mark. If the hidden parallels are valid, then Luke's use of Matthew becomes virtually impossible to deny.

But can we appeal to these hidden parallels to clinch the argument that Luke must have used Matthew? The obvious objection is that it's one thing for a modern interpreter to suggest hidden parallels between Matthew and Luke but quite another to show that they occurred to Luke. It's hard to know how this could be shown without reading Luke's mind, which is clearly impossible. But there are three points that go quite some way towards supporting Luke's deliberate use of these hidden parallels:

1. The alignment of Luke's sequence with Matthew's when the hidden parallels are taken into account.
2. The verbal similarities between some of the suggested parallels.
3. The ability of these parallels to explain Luke's sequence and potentially puzzling features of Luke's text.

Another objection might be the implausibility of Luke spinning so much material out of such slight hints in Matthew's text. There is, however, no need to suppose that this was what Luke was doing. It is more likely that, for the most part, these hidden parallels prompted Luke to use existing material (sometimes from Matthew, more often from his own special sources, such as a collection of parables). We shall return to this point below.

A third objection is that even if Luke's hidden parallels with Matthew might help to illuminate Luke's sequence, they still do not fully explain it, since we have yet to account for all the Matthean material Luke deploys out of Matthew's sequence. Some of this rearrangement might be prompted by the use of hidden parallels, but this is another point to which we shall return.

So far, we have covered only the first two steps in the argument about Luke's order. The remaining two steps are to ask how and why Luke may have worked in the manner we are proposing.

How Did Luke Do This?

As we saw in chapter 2, ancient authors lacked many of the tools we take for granted, and their working methods and compositional techniques weren't always the same as ours. Working with a handwritten scroll was very different from working with a printed text. If Luke was working from Matthew, he couldn't just skip from one passage to another by turning a few pages and looking things up by chapter and verse. Locating a passage by winding and unwinding a scroll was certainly possible, but compared with using a modern book, it would have been time consuming and laborious. We must next ask, then, how feasible it would have been for Luke to have used Matthew in the manner outlined above given the limitations of ancient writing technology and the compositional techniques ancient authors typically employed.

In many respects FH Luke's procedure is unproblematic. He will have used his two principal sources, Matthew and Mark, in alternating blocks (as can be seen in Columns A and C of Table 5.1). Prior to his central section, FH Luke's relocations of Markan and Matthean material are relatively modest, being no more extensive that Matthew's rearrangements of Mark. It's what happens when Luke embarks on his central section that looks rather more problematic. This poses two distinct questions: (a) how Luke could have reordered so much Matthean material across his central section and (b) how Luke could have transformed hidden parallels in Matthew to such seemingly different material in his own Gospel. We'll consider each of these questions in turn, but please remember that at this stage we're asking "how?" not "why?"

We may begin by reiterating a point we have already made. While FH Luke will have had to reorder quite a bit of Matthean material, the same applies to 2DH Matthew's reordering of Q. One might argue about the relative difficulty of these two cases, but even if they differ in difficulty at all (which is debatable), they hardly do so by an order of magnitude; what's possible for 2DH Matthew must also be possible for FH Luke.

That said, it is surely implausible to imagine Luke winding back and forth through a scroll of Matthew to pick up a verse here and a couple of verses there to insert into some completely different context in his own composition. We should therefore suppose that Luke's rearrangement of Matthew was achieved by some combination of the following (in roughly descending order of likely importance):

1. Luke most likely had good memory command of Matthew (as well as Mark) which allowed him to employ out-of-sequence Matthean extracts from memory. Most of these extracts (shown in Column B in Table 5.1) are taken from four of Matthew's five discourses: the Sermon on the Mount (Matt 5–7), the mission discourse (Matt 10), the parables discourse (Matt 13), and the woes against the scribes and Pharisees (Matt 23), four well-structured speeches of Jesus that Luke could well have committed to memory (given that memorization was practiced much more in antiquity than it is today), so that, having memorized them, it would not be too hard for him to scan them in his mind to extract the units he was after (which are always complete sense units, not isolated words or fragments).

2. Luke was unlikely to have been working in splendid isolation throughout the composition of his Gospel. He most likely dictated his first draft or drafts to a scribe and may well have had other collaborators. These persons' memories could have assisted his own.

3. It is likely that Luke's Gospel went through more than one draft before reaching the text we now have. Further rearrangement of Matthean material could have taken place in subsequent drafts, perhaps partly in response to feedback from the audiences of the earlier drafts. Luke need not necessarily have arrived at his rearrangement of Matthew all in one go.

4. As he worked through Matthew, Luke could have taken notes in a papyrus notebook or wax tablet (wooden sheets bound together and covered with wax that could be inscribed with a stylus). These need not have been complete extracts but could in principle have been brief memory prompts for material he planned to use at a later point, such as "Ask Seek Knock" as a prompt for Matt 7:7–11 (used at Luke 11:9–13). If Luke's memory command of Matthew's discourses was sufficiently good, he may not have needed such an aid, but on the other hand such brief notes could have helped him keep track of what Matthean material he had used.

The second issue is how (but not yet why) Luke could have picked up some often quite minor feature of a hidden parallel in Matthew and transformed it into what he wrote in his Gospel. How, for example, could a couple of verses Matthew added to Mark's account of picking grain on the Sabbath (Matt 12:5, 7) be transformed into the lawyer's question about the greatest commandment followed by the parable of the good Samaritan?

Here, "transformation" is probably the wrong word. Luke has most likely borrowed the initial question and answer from Mark 12:28–34 and the parable that follows from some other source, either oral tradition or a written parable collection. The hidden parallels suggested at Luke 11:39–52; 14:25–27; and 17:6 similarly involve Luke's redeployment of existing material (in these three cases taken from elsewhere in Matthew) into a new context. Those at Luke 14:7–24; 16:1–12; 16:19–31; and 18:1–8 could similarly have come about through Luke's drawing on an existing parable collection, sometimes in conjunction with borrowings from other parts of Matthew. Luke may well have adapted his source material to its new context, but the extent to which he engaged in wholesale invention on the basis of slender hints may be fairly limited. In the main, the hints Matthew's hidden parallels provided would have been memory cues prompting Luke's use of existing material.

The proposal, then, is that for the most part Luke's use of hidden parallels occur when, in the course of his working forwards through Matthew, some feature of the Matthean text prompts Luke's recollection of other material he decides to use at the corresponding point in his own composition. Leaving aside for the moment the question *why* he might choose to work like this, the question *how* then relates principally to the workings of Luke's memory, which are no longer accessible to us. What we can say is that, in general, human memory often works by associative cueing, of which this would be one example. Associative cueing was a common feature of biblical and other ancient writings (the chain of quotations at Rom 3:10-18 is but one of many such examples, whether it was compiled by Paul or by some earlier writer). There is thus no inherent mechanical or psychological implausibility in what we are proposing here. Beyond that we can only speculate, for example on what kind of debating, preaching, or teaching activity Luke may have engaged in that helped form particular memory links in his brain. But in any case, we are not suggesting that Luke simply followed random associations that happened to be triggered by what he came across in Matthew; we should rather envisage him engaged in a kind of mental dialogue with the Matthean text in which the associations Luke finds are influenced by the topics he wishes to pursue.

That said, we have already suggested that Luke is also capable of some quite creative imitation (for example in his infancy narratives, but also in Luke 4:16-30 and 7:11—8:3) and this could well be how he worked in the case of some of the other hidden parallels, such as those at Luke 9:52-56; 13:31-33; and 17:11-19, in which instances the Matthean hidden parallel may not have been his sole model. For example, Luke's story of the healing of the ten lepers may have drawn on the story of the healing of a leper at Mark 1:40-45 along with the healing of Naaman in 2 Kgs 5, which Luke explicitly references in Jesus' inaugural sermon at Luke 4:27. In both cases Luke draws attention to the healing of a non-Israelite leper, and just as the Samaritan leper returns to thank Jesus at Luke 17:15-18, so does the Syrian leper return to thank Elisha at 2 Kgs 5:15.

Why Did Luke Do This?

The question *why* Luke would have worked with Matthew in this way is more complex and comes up against the difficulty that we cannot read Luke's mind. The best we can do is to suggest reasonably plausible motives that are reasonably consistent with what Luke does elsewhere and with the kinds of thing an ancient author might have aimed for.

The question why Luke did what he did resolves into three sub-questions, the first two of which are commonly raised as objections to Luke's use of Matthew: (1) Why did Luke break up Matthew's Sermon on the Mount (scattering fragments of it elsewhere)? (2) What was Luke up to in his central section (where he mixes special material of his own with material taken from all over the place in Matthew)? And (3) Why would Luke make use of the hidden parallels with Matthew suggested above? We shall now tackle each of these sub-questions in turn, leading to a final assessment of what FH Luke will have been doing with Matthew.

Luke's Treatment of the Sermon on the Mount

Matthew's Sermon on the Mount occupies three chapters (5–7) of Matthew's Gospel. Luke's equivalent, the Sermon on the Plain, takes up roughly two-thirds of a single chapter (Luke 6:20–49) of his. Apart from a couple of verses borrowed from later in Matthew, nearly all the material in Luke's sermon parallels material in Matthew's, but a great deal of Matthew's sermon is either omitted from Luke altogether or deployed in quite different contexts, mainly distributed across Luke's central section. The question is often asked why Luke would mutilate Matthew's fine sermon in this way.

Posing the question in this way presupposes value judgments we have no reason to believe Luke shared. Luke may or may not have admired Matthew's Sermon on the Mount, but it would be anachronistic to assume that either he or the church of his day regarded it as the classic statement of Jesus' teaching that it has come to be seen as in subsequent Christian tradition, and it's extremely unlikely that he regarded the composition of his own, shorter, version as an act of mutilation. Budding writers and budding orators were taught a variety of techniques, which included both expanding and contracting their models. They would also be taught a number of literary virtues to aim for, some of which might conflict with one another, but which would certainly include clarity, conciseness, and appropriateness.

An Orderly Account?

From Luke's perspective, the Sermon on the Plain improves on the Sermon on the Mount on all three counts. By focusing on the points Luke wants to emphasize most, his version of the sermon gains in both clarity and conciseness. By omitting material Luke would likely regard as less relevant to his target audience, he also makes it more appropriate to its context and purpose. It is not so much that Luke has some consistent aesthetic preference for short speeches (although the Sermon on the Mount would be considerably longer than any speech in Luke-Acts, and Luke nearly always shortens the speeches he adapts from Matthew and Mark), but that in this context the shorter speech he assigns to Jesus at this point in his narrative is more rhetorically effective in relation to Luke's aims.

Matthew's Sermon on the Mount constitutes Jesus' first set-piece speech in the Gospel of Matthew. But Luke's Sermon on the Plain is Jesus' second speech in his, the first being the Nazareth sermon at Luke 4:16–30. The Nazareth Sermon opens with Luke proclaiming the fulfillment of Isa 61:1–2a. This in turn starts with the speaker saying that he has been anointed to preach good news to the poor, which is precisely what Jesus does at the start of Luke's Sermon on the Plain: "Happy the poor, because yours is the kingdom of God" (Luke 6:20). After contrasting the fate of the currently rich and poor (in terms that recall Mary's Song at Luke 1:51–53), Luke's sermon goes to focus on non-retaliation, generosity, refraining from judgment, and behaving with sincerity. These are all themes Luke emphasizes elsewhere, and which could also be seen as consonant with the Isaiah citation at Luke 4:18–19. That Luke has the Nazareth sermon in mind in this section of the Gospel is suggested by the material immediately following the Sermon on the Plain. The healing of the Capernaum centurion (Luke 7:1–10) and the healing of Naaman the leper (2 Kgs 5) referenced at Luke 4:27 both concern the healing of a foreign military officer, while the raising of the widow's son at Nain (Luke 7:11–17) recalls the raising of the widow's son at Zarephath (1 Kgs 17:8–24), referenced at Luke 4:26.

Much of the material Luke omits from the Sermon on the Mount could well be considered inappropriate to a gentile audience, not least since it largely concerns interpretations of the Jewish Torah (Matt 5:19–37) or the practice of Jewish forms of piety (Matt 6:1–6, 16–18). The two sections of Matthew's antitheses (contrasts between ancient interpretations of the Law and Jesus') that Luke does retain (Luke 6:27–36 || Matt 5:38–48) are recast so that they are no longer presented as contrasting interpretations of the Torah, but simply as Jesus' teaching on non-retaliation and love of enemies. The opening words of Luke 6:27, "But to those who hear I say, love your enemies" read a little oddly after Luke 6:26, "Alas for you when all people speak well of you, for their ancestors did the same to the false prophets," since it is less than immediately clear what contrast Luke has in mind. The contrast is rather clearer in the corresponding passage at Matt 5:43–44 where "You have heard that it was said, 'You shall hate your enemy and love your neighbor'" is immediately contrasted with, "But I say to you, love your enemy . . . ," creating the suspicion that Luke may have adapted Matthew just a little clumsily here, with "You have heard that it was said . . . But I say to you" altered to "But to those who hear I say."

Luke reserves the remainder of Matthew chapter 6 (6:9–13, 19–34) and parts of Matthew chapter 7 (7:7–11, 13–14, 22–23) for use in his central section, where it is placed in a variety of different contexts. Why he does so belongs more to a discussion of Luke's central section than to one about his Sermon on the Plain, beyond the point already made about Luke focusing the Sermon on a smaller range of topics. It may nevertheless be noted that the Matthean material thus relocated largely concerns topics Luke will go on to develop in his central section, such as prayer (Matt 6:9–13), the perils of riches (Matt 6:19–24) and corresponding reliance on God for basic needs (Matt 6:25–34; 7:7–11).

Luke's Central Section

Luke's central section (also referred to as his travel narrative) has long presented something of a puzzle. It contains a good deal of sayings material, not least many parables unique to Luke, interspersed with a few short incidents, including three healing stories and various encounters with people Jesus comes across, some friendly, such as Martha and Mary, and others hostile, such as various Pharisees and other representatives of the Jewish establishment. It opens at a clear turning point in Luke's Gospel at Luke 9:51, with Jesus setting out on his final journey to Jerusalem. It then appears to meander for several chapters with only a few clear indications of movement until Jesus finally arrives at Jerusalem for the triumphal entry in Luke 19:28. It is unclear whether to count the central section as ending there, or at 18:14, or at some point in between.

The section that primarily interests us here is the one running from Luke 9:51 to 18:14, which contains a mixture of Double Tradition and L material, in other words, material FH Luke would have taken from

Matthew and material unique to himself (with only the very occasional echo of Mark). After 18:14 Luke resumes following Mark once more (except for the passage about Jesus' encounter with the tax collector Zacchaeus at Luke 19:1-10). The difficulty is to discern why Luke might have chosen to arrange his central section as he did.

To some extent this remains a problem on any theory of synoptic relationships, since many scholars have found the rationale behind the arrangement of the central section less than immediately apparent. The 2DH can claim that Luke was simply following the order of Q for the material he shares with Matthew, but that still doesn't explain why he would have interspersed his Q and L material in quite the way he did. The FH has the additional burden of having to explain why Luke used quite so much Matthean material out of its Matthean order and context (see Table 5.1 above).

That said, Luke's central section is by no means totally shapeless. It starts with a coherent enough narrative opening: Jesus sets out for Jerusalem, presumably with the intention of confronting the nation's leadership (9:51) and sends messengers out ahead of him, presumably to prepare the way by announcing the message of the coming kingdom (9:52). The messengers strike south through Samaria but are rejected, causing Jesus to continue via another route (9:52-56). Along the way he encounters would-be disciples (9:57-62) and then sends seventy others out to proclaim the coming of the kingdom (10:1-16) apparently with some measure of success (10:17-24). It's after that point that the narrative thread peters out, at least until the end of the section, where there appears to be some recapitulation of themes introduced near the beginning; for example, the one grateful Samaritan leper in 17:11-19 reverses the hostile reception Jesus received from Samaritans right at the start and recalls the good Samaritan of the parable at 10:30-36, while the short block on prayer (18:1-14) recalls the earlier block on prayer (11:1-13) along with other themes that have recurred throughout the central section, including critique of Pharisees (11:37—12:3 and frequently thereafter), God's acceptance of the humble penitent (especially Luke 15 but elsewhere as well) and the coming of the kingdom (Luke 17:20-37 but elsewhere as well).

These themes, plus one or two others, such as the demands of discipleship, the perils of riches, and repentance in preparation for the coming judgement, occupy the bulk of Jesus' teaching in this section. Often such themes extend over substantial blocks, as we have seen (another example would be the substantial block on preparing for Jesus' return and the coming judgment at 12:35—13:9). Sometimes (as we have already seen at 18:1–14) a block may be concerned with more than one theme. Occasionally, other themes relevant to discipleship appear, such as the love command as the greatest commandment (10:25-37) or the proper use of hospitality (14:12–14), although the latter of these could be counted as a specific example of the proper use of wealth.

At this point it may be helpful to list some of the more plausible suggestions for the overall design and purpose of Luke's central section. These are by no means mutually exclusive; they could well all be true, and some of them don't depend on any particular theory of synoptic relationships (where they do, I'll make it clear by referring to FH Luke).

1. Luke wished to gather the bulk of Jesus' teaching (on the themes in question) into one main section in his Gospel, between the two narrative sections with which he begins and ends, but to do so in a way that creates the impression of ongoing narrative movement while in fact being largely comprised of sayings of Jesus.

2. Mark Goodacre has suggested that FH Luke wished to preserve the Markan "Way of the Lord" motif. This is particularly prominent in Mark's central section (Mark 8:27—11:2), which mostly involves Jesus' journey to Jerusalem. The centrality of this section is largely obscured in Matthew, largely as a result of Matthew's arrangement of much of Jesus' teaching into five discourses, four of which occur in Jesus' Galilean ministry before Matthew's Jesus sets out for Jerusalem at Matt 19:1. The result is that Matthew's account of the journey to Jerusalem becomes a far smaller proportion of the whole and no longer occupies a pivotal position. Yet FH Luke also wanted to make use of much of the additional material in Matthew's extended Galilean ministry. Luke's long central section represents his attempt to preserve both Mark's Way of the Lord theme with a central travel section and valuable material from Matthew's extended Galilean ministry, resulting in the relocation of much of Matthew's Galilean material to a different sequence in Luke's central section.

3. The announcement that Jesus "set his face" to go to Jerusalem indicates not just that he was determined to go there, but that he would be coming to the symbolic center of Israel for confrontation and judgment. The central section then leads up to this by showing Jesus, on the one hand, gathering the nucleus of a new people of God (and

instructing them in discipleship) and, on the other, meeting increasing opposition and rejection from the official representatives of ethnic Israel (such as scribes, lawyers, Pharisees, and leaders of synagogues). This prepares the way both for Jesus' death and resurrection when he reaches Jerusalem and for the gentile mission in Acts. It also acts christologically to portray Jesus as the expected prophet like Moses of Deut 18:15–19 who, as the culmination of a long line of prophets, is destined to meet the same rejection by Israel as they did (cf. Acts 3:17–26; 7:35–37, 51–53).

4. Relocating Matthean material to different contexts allows FH Luke to give it a different slant. For example, in Matthew, the passage about would-be disciples comes in the middle of Jesus' Galilean ministry just as Jesus is about to board a boat to cross the Sea of Galilee (Matt 8:18–22), whereas by placing it near the start of his central section (at Luke 9:57–62) and prefacing it with a notice that Jesus and his disciples were going along the road, Luke both integrates it into his travel theme and uses it to introduce the theme of the demands of discipleship that will feature repeatedly in what follows. Or again, in its Matthean context, the Lord's Prayer (Matt 6:9–13) is presented as part of a polemical contrast with misguided ways of praying, whereas in its Lukan context (Luke 11:2–4) it becomes part of a section on teaching in prayer offered in response to a request from Jesus' disciples. Or, as a final example, by relocating the sections on anxiety and on treasure in heaven (Matt 6:25–34, 19–21) to a position immediately following the L warning against avarice and parable of the rich fool (Luke 12:22–31), FH Luke makes the adapted Matthean material more clearly function as part of his own critique of reliance on riches.

Luke's central section is not, after all, some mere rag-bag into which FH Luke has scattered material torn from the Sermon on the Mount and elsewhere in Matthew into random contexts having no special appropriateness, but rather a composition with its own logic and purpose. Admittedly, some elements of Luke's design remain obscure. While one can trace some sort of narrative and thematic sequence across his central section, some transitions remain unexplained and the precise structuring principle is often far from clear. Or, to put it another way, Luke's sequence in his central section seems underdetermined by the considerations we have suggested so far, although it does appear designed to foreground certain topics (as we have seen).

This, however, may be more of a strength than a weakness for the case being made here, since the very fact that the structure of Luke's central section seems not wholly determined by Luke's narrative, theological and thematic aims leaves scope for another principle also to be at work, and that principle could well be FH Luke's broadly following the Matthean sequence identified in Table 5.2 above.

Why Would Luke Make Use of Hidden Parallels?

We are accordingly proposing that Luke's order is partly guided by Matthew's, especially in his central section where the rationale of Luke's order may not otherwise be fully apparent. That Luke's obvious parallels to material he shares with Matthew should sometimes occur in the same sequence in both Gospels is not particularly surprising if Luke is using Matthew. But we suggested above that Matthew's influence on Luke's order extends beyond this to instances in which features of Matthew's text influence Luke's choice of material where FH Luke would be continuing to follow Matthew roughly in Matthew's sequence. We have termed these instances "hidden parallels" since they are not the kind of clear and obvious parallels that occur in the (more or less) undisputed Matthew/Luke Double Tradition. In these instances, Luke would not simply have copied, adapted, or paraphrased Matthew, but would rather have used Matthew's text as a jumping off point for his own composition.

That these hidden parallels exist (in some sense) is not in question; we have already shown that they are present in the text and that they fill out a sequence of parallels between Luke and Matthew in a roughly common order. What may be questioned is whether Luke intended these hidden parallels or whether they are merely the product of a modern interpreter's ingenuity. That the hidden parallels sometimes exhibit verbal links between the two Gospels and sometimes help explain what might otherwise be puzzling in Luke lends some support to their being intentional, but the case for their being so would be strengthened further if plausible reasons can be offered *why* Luke might have employed them.

Certainty is impossible here, since certainty would require us to read Luke's mind, but we may nevertheless offer several possible reasons for Luke's use of hidden Matthean parallels:

An Orderly Account?

1. Luke was in any case working sequentially forward through Matthew and had a good idea of the kind of material he wanted to include in his central section. Where something in Matthew's Gospel sparked an association with something Luke intended to use in any case, he found it expedient to take advantage of the association to guide his own sequencing of material where it was otherwise undetermined by his own compositional design. Often Luke used such associations to guide his deployment of material taken from elsewhere in Matthew.

2. Luke wished to make as much use of Matthew as he could within the constraints of his own compositional aims. Many of the hidden parallels occur where Luke could not employ Matthew directly because Matthew was using Markan passages Luke deployed elsewhere (or did not want to make direct use of at all). Exploiting hidden parallels in these cases allowed Luke to use or develop valuable Matthean teaching on, for example, preferring mercy to sacrifice (added by Matthew to the Markan story about plucking grain on the Sabbath) or faith (prompted by the story of the withering of the fig tree Luke otherwise omits).

3. We have seen Luke make imitative use of Matthew elsewhere in his Gospel (notably in the infancy narratives and possibly in the resurrection narratives as well). Literary (or rhetorical) imitation was often closely associated with *emulation*, the attempt to rival and improve on one's model. Luke's central section could be viewed as an emulation of the corresponding section of Matthew (which, according to Table 5.2 above, would comprise Matt 8:19—25:30, although with minimal use of sections such as the passion narrative where Luke and Matthew are primarily using Mark). Luke's use of hidden parallels could then be seen as part of this emulation, providing Luke with the means to include material that is similar in kind to that found in Matthew while varying from it in specific content (sometimes through Luke substituting his own material, and sometimes through his deploying material from elsewhere in Matthew's Gospel).

These possibilities are mutually compatible and mutually overlapping. Let us now think about the last of them in a bit more detail.

We are suggesting that Luke set out to emulate Matthew (and Mark), where emulation is a form of competitive imitation. There were no set rules for how to go about imitating a model in antiquity; techniques could range from paraphrase or even a modicum of quotation through imitation of features of style, structure, or content to an attempt to capture the spirit of the original. FH Luke would seem to have employed the full spectrum of such techniques. His broad aim in doing so would have been to offer a portrait of Jesus that was recognizably the same figure as that presented in his main sources but reshaped to express his own concerns and ideals to his target audience. In doing this he will have been concerned to both transmit and transform the tradition available to him (Luke 1:1–4). Where he can use material from Matthew or Mark virtually unchanged, he does so. Where he needs to exercise considerable artistic license to get his point across, he appears willing to do that also (as, almost unmistakably, at Luke 4:20–30 and 5:1–11, but also in several other places we have observed).

On this model, FH Luke's use of hidden parallels from Matthew forms part of his wider project of emulation, with the precise aim varying in individual cases. Sometimes he may wish to correct Matthew (e.g., Matt 10:5 → Luke 9:52–56). Sometimes he may want to improve on him by substituting his own material on similar themes (e.g., Matt 13:1–50→ Luke 12:16—13:30; Matt 18:23–34 → Luke 16:1–12). Sometimes he may take the opportunity to emphasize one of his own favorite themes when he encounters a Matthean passage he intends to use elsewhere (Matt 19:16–22 → Luke 16:19–31). Sometimes he'll use elements from a Matthean parallel to Mark in a narrative sequence of his own (Matt 14:1–21 → Luke 13:31–33; 14:7–24). Sometimes he'll do something different again. Often, he won't simply create his own material afresh but draw it in from elsewhere in Matthew (Matt 12:33–37 → Luke 11:39–52, drawing mainly on Matt 23:4–36), or on his own store of material (such as the uniquely Lukan parables).

More broadly, FH Luke's aim is to emulate both Matthew and Mark. He imitates the Markan structure (and Way of the Lord theme) by including a significant central section focused on Jesus' final journey to Jerusalem, but improves on it by incorporating a good deal of valuable material from Matthew (and elsewhere). At the same time, he imitates Matthew by incorporating a good deal of valuable material from Matthew's Gospel while improving on it (at least in Luke's view) by placing it within a structure borrowed from Mark. Luke's imitation of Matthew extends to including a great deal of material that is similar in kind to that found in Matthew even when it is not exactly the same material, such as Jesus teaching disciples and crowds, engaging in debate with Pharisees and other Jewish authority figures, and carrying out the occasional healing. The use of hidden parallels would be an aid to Luke's employment of a broadly similar mix of materials even when the details differ, while the redeployment of material out of its Matthean sequence (such as material taken from the Sermon on the Mount and other Matthean discourses) further strengthens the resemblance between the Jesus of Luke's central section and Matthew's Jesus. By emulating both Mark and Matthew in this way, Luke aims to present a Jesus who will be acceptable to audiences for whom Mark and Matthew are authoritative while also serving Luke's aims and ideals.

How plausible this account will seem depends largely on what sort of author one takes Luke to be. It will seem fanciful to anyone who sees Luke as a mere compiler and transmitter of tradition employing his sources in straightforward copy and edit mode. It is hard to see, however, how such a Luke could have composed infancy narratives so clearly imitative of the Old Testament (let alone Matthew), or accounts of a rejection at Nazareth sermon (Luke 4:16–30) or the call of the first disciples (Luke 5:1–11) so extensively developed from their apparent Markan parallels (Mark 6:1–6; 1:16–20; 4:1), or the account of a trial before Herod (Luke 23:6–12), apparently borrowing elements from Mark 15:2–5, 16–19; 6:14–16. Older scholarship was wont to attribute such Lukan divergences from Mark to Luke's use of an alternative source or sources (such as an L-source), but there is absolutely no evidence for the existence of any such source in these instances apart from the assumption that Luke was an author of such limited creativity that he was capable of nothing more than copying and editing his sources. But there is nothing to warrant such an assumption, which merely pushes back the problem of creativity to Luke's hypothetical sources. It certainly isn't warranted by the (largely conventional) claims made at Luke 1:1–4, which mean, not that Luke has carried out a thorough historical investigation and arranged the results in chronological order, but that he is steeped in the tradition handed down from "the eyewitnesses and ministers of the word" and is undertaking to shape them into an appropriate literary order. This tells us little, if anything, about the degree of artistic license Luke felt free to exercise in order to convey his own interpretation of "the things fulfilled among us," and it would be anachronistic to assume that what Luke regarded as an acceptable balance between precise fidelity to empirical fact and appropriate literary reshaping to bring out theological significance would closely resemble that of modern historians. In any case the only good evidence we have of Luke's literary abilities are the writings he has left us (his Gospel and Acts). To argue that any indications in these writings that Luke could do more than copy and edit must be illusory because we know Luke was incapable of anything more would be perversely circular, especially since the evidence suggests otherwise.

Summary

The argument from order is often taken to be the most telling argument against Luke's use of Matthew, on the basis that it would have made no sense for Luke to have broken up Matthew's discourses, especially the Sermon on the Mount, and scatter the material over his central section to little apparent purpose, and that it would have been mechanically cumbersome for him to do so if it meant having to constantly wind and unwind a scroll of Matthew to pick out the Matthean fragments he wanted to redeploy. The current chapter has countered this argument in several stages:

1. The mechanical difficulty involved in FH Luke's use of Matthew is no greater than that involved in 2DH Matthew's use of Q. In both cases the difficulty would most likely have been overcome through the writer's memory command of his sources. Luke need only have known four of Matthew's discourses by heart to have accessed from memory the bulk of the Matthean material he deployed elsewhere in his own composition.

2. FH Luke might quite reasonably have wished to abbreviate Matthew's Sermon on the Mount to his own Sermon on the Plain. A shorter speech focusing on a few key issues could well be more rhetorically effective.

3. Despite the initial appearance of wayward reordering of Matthean material, FH Luke in fact worked steadily forward through Matthew from beginning to end. The correspondence in order between the Gospels becomes even more apparent when Luke's use of hidden parallels in Matthew is included.

4. Luke's central section is not a random ragbag of ill-assorted material, but a composition focusing on a limited number of themes set in a presentation of Jesus on the way to Jerusalem (in imitation of the way of the Lord theme in Mark) and showing, on the one hand, the way of discipleship and the gathering of a new people of God, and on

the other, the opposition of the leading representatives of the Jewish people, which will lead to Jesus' rejection in Jerusalem.

5. FH Luke's procedure makes good sense on the basis that he set out to emulate his two predecessor Gospels (in order to rival if not supplant them while reclaiming their authority for his own point of view).

Some people may regard the proposals for hidden parallels put forward here as being novel and unpersuasive, the product of modern ingenuity rather than Luke's intention. Indeed, proponents of the 2DH will be almost bound to see them in this light, since to concede the validity of the hidden parallels would be to concede Luke's of Matthew; they form a set of sequential parallels between Luke and Matthew that cannot be explained by Q and are often dependent on Matthean redaction of Mark. But even if every single hidden parallel proposed above were to be dismissed as wholly fanciful, the other arguments would remain, and Luke's reordering of Matthew will still have been defended as plausible. The contribution of the hidden parallels is to advance Luke's use of Matthew from plausible to virtually inescapable. To object that the structure of Luke's central section remains obscure is to overstate its apparent shapelessness, but to recognize that is undetermined by other considerations is to concede the explanatory power the hidden parallels can offer by increasing the extent to which Matthew's order can be seen to have influenced Luke's.

6

Conclusion

THE PURPOSE OF THIS book has been to introduce the case for the Farrer Hypothesis. It has not aimed to give the reader a neutral and objective evaluation of every conceivable solution to the Synoptic Problem, or even just the more common ones. Neither has it attempted to go into every nook and cranny of the often complex sets of similarities and differences between the three Synoptic Gospels. And rather than claiming to introduce *the* case for the Farrer Hypothesis, it should more modestly claim to offer *a* case. Although those of us who advocate the Farrer Hypothesis make use of many of the same arguments, we each have our own individual slant. So, for example, while the argument about Luke's sequential use of hidden parallels in Matthew presented in chapter 5 draws on the insights of earlier scholars such as Michael Goulder, to the best of my knowledge the form in which I've presented it is peculiar to me, and though I'm hardly alone in suggesting that Luke made use of literary/rhetorical imitation, my particular proposals for Luke's emulation of Matthew may be relatively novel.

The case made here involves the following interlocking arguments:

1. The extent of similarity in wording and order between Matthew, Mark, and Luke is best explained on the basis of some form of literary relationship between them.

2. A number of considerations taken together point to Mark being the earliest of these three Gospels and an important source for the other two. These include the relatively unliterary nature of Mark's Greek compared to the other two, the difficulty of explaining why Mark would have omitted so much from Matthew and/or Luke, the mechanical

Conclusion

difficulty Mark would have faced in attempting to combine Matthew and Luke in the manner envisaged by the Two Gospel Hypothesis, and the various examples of editorial fatigue, where seemingly odd features of Matthew and Luke are best explained as due to their failing to carry through their adaptations of Mark consistently.

3. If we could be sure that neither Matthew nor Luke knew or used the other, then we should need to find some other way to account for the material they have in common that is not found in Mark (the so-called Double Tradition). The most economical way of doing this would be to suppose that they had independent access to a second source, which modern scholarship calls Q. The Two Document Hypothesis that results would then be the most robust solution to the Synoptic Problem.

4. But when the arguments against Luke's use of Matthew are examined, they turn out to be not nearly so convincing as advocates of the Two Document Hypothesis maintain. If it's reasonable to suppose that Luke could have used Matthew after all, there is no need to postulate the existence of a further hypothetical source Q. Instead it becomes preferable to suppose that Matthew used Mark and that Luke subsequently used the other two. (It is also conceivable that Matthew came last in such a scenario, but there are more places where Luke appears secondary to Matthew than vice versa).

5. There are similarities between Matthew and Luke that cannot be explained by their independent use of Mark and Q. This includes their respective openings (in which Luke appears to have partly imitated and partly copied Matthew) and a substantial number of agreements of Matthew and Luke against Mark. Taken together these similarities between Matthew and Luke make a direct relationship between them not only plausible but highly probable.

6. The most telling objection to Luke's use of Matthew is often taken to be Luke's substantial reordering of much of the material he would have taken from Matthew. Against that it should be recognized that a similar objection could be raised against Matthew's reordering of Q. In both cases much of the difficulty can be alleviated by supposing that Luke and Matthew had good memory command of their sources. The bulk of the material Luke redistributes from Matthew comes from four of the five Matthean discourses, limiting the quantity of material

Luke would need to scan in memory to retrieve what he wishes to place in a different context. Despite this rearrangement, the order of Luke's composition is broadly guided by that of his principal sources, Mark and Matthew (especially when Luke's use of hidden parallels is taken into account).

7. Another objection to Luke's use of Matthew is that it would require Luke to work in a way uncharacteristic of other ancient authors. But that objection loses its force if we don't confine Luke to being a mere copy-and-edit compiler of tradition. Like other ancient authors, the Luke envisaged here mainly follows one source at a time, alternating between blocks where he uses Matthew and blocks where he uses Mark. He does not follow a simply copy-and-edit mode of composition but employs a variety of transformational techniques (such as paraphrase, expansion, contraction, and elaboration) commonly taught as part of a literate education. He sometimes employs more creative forms of literary imitation, which are also found in other ancient authors (and which can be recognized in Luke's use of the Old Testament). He does so because his aim is not to simply rehash his sources, but to emulate them, that is to produce a Gospel that it is a competitive imitation of his predecessors, to rival and displace them but also to borrow their authority in service of his own views.

Although I believe this case to be a strong one, the reader should be warned that not everyone will agree. Advocates of other source-critical theories will doubtless pick holes in it, for example by suggesting sets of Synoptic parallels they believe the Farrer Hypothesis struggles to explain. This is partly because, as we said at the outset, there is no theory of synoptic relationships that is demonstrably free of all difficulties; if there were, we would not still be debating the Synoptic Problem. It is also because many of the arguments on all sides of the debate inevitably involve some element of subjective judgment, however fair and objective we strive to be. What strikes one person as conclusive may strike another as wholly unconvincing. Different people will have different estimates of plausibility. One person's striking similarity may be another's vague resemblance. Conflicting evidence may be weighed differently by different people. Different scholars will have different views on the level of Luke's literary skill (say) and hence on where to seek appropriate ancient parallels to his working methods. More generally, we all have our inbuilt cognitive biases, not least confirmation bias:

Conclusion

the tendency to be persuaded by arguments that favor positions we already hold and to find arguments to the contrary unconvincing.

That said, there is a tendency among some introductory treatments to the Synoptic Problem to treat the Two Document Hypothesis as almost self-evidently correct and to keep repeating the same arguments against competing solutions without any apparent acknowledgment that defenders of those solutions have long since come up with counterarguments. If this introduction does nothing else, it should at least help you to become aware of the main counterarguments offered by the Farrer Hypothesis, and hence to be wary of any advocacy for the Two Document Hypothesis that fails to engage with them.

Finally, remember that any proposed solution to the Synoptic Problem can only be a model, not a complete account of everything that actually went into the composition of the three Synoptic Gospels. The Farrer Hypothesis is hopefully a good model, in that it offers reasonable simplicity and hence usability, but at best it can only be a reasonable approximation to what actually happened. Nevertheless, it is hopefully a good enough approximation for most practical purposes, rather as Newtonian mechanics is a good enough approximation for most practical purposes, unless we are dealing with the very small (for which we need quantum mechanics) or the very fast or very large (for which we need relativity).

This analogy is not exact, of course, since the reasons any tolerably simple model of synoptic relations may only approximate what actually happened are quite different in kind from those that apply to Newtonian mechanics. As noted in chapter 1, what actually happened almost certainly involved a number of messy complexities that cannot be reconstructed, such as multiple stages in composition, textual variations introduced in the course of copying manuscripts, and the use of additional sources now lost to us, some written, some oral, and many perhaps involving an intricate interplay between memory, manuscript, and speech.

For some people, awareness of such complexities means we should abandon the attempt to formulate any straightforward solution to the Synoptic Problem, although sometimes this can seem like a rhetorical strategy for leaving the Two Document Hypothesis in place by simultaneously dismissing challenges to it for illegitimately ignoring the complexities and appealing to the same complexities to account for any difficulties with the Two Document Hypothesis (such as agreements of Matthew and Luke against Mark). For others, awareness of complexity acts as an invitation to devise more complex theories involving multiple hypothetical sources. It may be impossible to disprove such theories, but that is their weakness: the more complex they become the harder it becomes to either verify or falsify them, let alone to work with them. It is surely better to resort to more complex theories only if and when simpler theories have been tested to destruction. The case made here is that the Farrer Hypothesis is better able to withstand such testing than its principal competitors, not least the still dominant Two Document Hypothesis.

Appendix

Suggestions for Further Reading

THE PUBLISHED LITERATURE ON the Synoptic Problem is extensive. A limited selection of suggestions for further reading is given here not with any expectation that readers will want to look at them all, but rather (a) to indicate some of the sources of the ideas and arguments covered and (b) to allow readers to follow up any points they're particularly interested in. Items listed for each topic are arranged roughly from more introductory to more specialized. Full details of the publications mentioned are given in the bibliography.

In addition to the suggestions given below, note that the arguments covered in the present book are treated in considerably more depth and detail in my book *Relating the Gospels* (which is aimed at an audience more familiar with the academic study of the New Testament).

Chapter 1 - Introduction

No introduction to the Synoptic Problem is written from a purely neutral perspective, since virtually everyone who writes on it favors one solution or another.

Porter and Dyers, *Synoptic Problem*, contains relatively brief defenses of four main solutions to the Synoptic Problem by advocates of various positions.

Sanders and Davies, *Studying the Synoptic Gospels*, 51–119, give a useful overview of the Synoptic Problem. They end up tending towards a qualified Farrer view.

Relatively brief introductions to the Synoptic Problem from a 2DH perspective can be found in Tuckett, "Current State"; Tuckett, *Q and the History of Early Christianity*, 1–39; and Kloppenborg, *Excavating Q*, 11–54.

For a brief book-length introduction from the Farrer perspective see Goodacre, *Synoptic Problem*. For a chapter-length survey sympathetic to the FH see Eve, "Synoptic Problem without Q?" See also the classic statement in Farrer, "On Dispensing with Q."

For the Two Gospel Hypothesis see Farmer, *Synoptic Problem*; for a critique see Tuckett, *Revival*.

Brief statements of the Matthean Posteriority Hypothesis can be found in Huggins, "Matthean Posteriority" and Hengel, *Four Gospels*, 169–207. For a more sustained treatment, see MacEwen, *Matthean Posteriority*.

For the Synoptic Problem as involving a literary relationship between texts, see Gregory, "What is Literary Dependence?" For challenges to the so-called "literary paradigm" see Dunn, "Altering the Default Setting" and the critique of Dunn in Kloppenborg, "Variation and Reproduction."

For the hypothetical nature of solutions to the Synoptic Problem, see Kloppenborg, "Conceptual Stakes."

Chapter 2–Gospel Writing in the First Century

How Ancient Writers Worked

For a general introduction to the Evangelists' and other ancient authors' working methods, see Eve, *Writing the Gospels* and Derrenbacker, "The 'External and Psychological Conditions under which the Synoptic Gospels Were Written.'" For more advanced discussions, see Derrenbacker, *Ancient Compositional Practices*; Gamble, *Books and Readers* and Winsbury, *Roman Book*.

Transforming Sources

It's hard to find any single introductory level treatment that covers all the ways in which ancient authors might adapt their source material. Downing's articles, "Redaction Criticism I" and "Redaction Criticism II" offer a useful first foray into this area, but arguably don't give the full picture. Pelling's articles, "Plutarch's Method of Work" and "Plutarch's Adaptation" have been much cited by New Testament scholars working in this area and are well worth a look.

Readers interested in how ancient rhetorical education and practice informed the way in which ancient authors' might typically adapt their source material might like to consult Kennedy, *Progymnasmata* and Damm, *Ancient Rhetoric*.

For introductory discussions on the use of *memory* in composition see Eve, *Writing the Gospel*, 81–102 and Gregory, "What is Literary Dependence?," 95–103.

Kirk, *Q in Matthew*, contains thorough discussions both of the use of memory in composition and in the ways in which it may have aided some kind of reordering of source material, but this book cannot be regarded as remotely introductory. Non-specialist readers may prefer to sample his work in this area in his essay on "Memory, Scribal Media, and the Synoptic Problem."

For an introduction to ancient *literary imitation* in general, see Russel, "De Imitatione." For an introduction to Virgil's imitation of Homer, see Knauer, "Vergil's *Aeneid* and Homer" (but this may be more useful to readers with at least a rudimentary knowledge of the contents of Homer's and Virgil's epics). For the application of imitation (or mimesis criticism) to the New Testament (and, to some extent, the Synoptic Problem), see Winn, *Mark and the Elijah-Elisha Narrative*; McAdon, *Rhetorical Mimesis*; O'Leary, *Matthew's Judaization*; and MacDonald (ed.), *Mimesis and Intertextuality*. Readers wishing to delve deeper into the mimesis criticism of the New Testament might like to look at Brodie, *Birthing* and MacDonald, *The Gospels and Homer*, but may wish to do so with a critical eye. For MacDonald at his most convincing see "The Shipwrecks of Odysseus and Paul." While Michael Goulder does not use the term "imitation," the compositional techniques he describes at *Luke*, 105–7 are akin to those other authors identify as typical of literary imitation.

For the reasons people might have for writing a gospel, see Eve, *Writing the Gospels*, 20–38. For the genre of the gospels being that of *bios* (the ancient equivalent of biography), see Burridge, *What Are the Gospels?* For a substantial discussion of what that might mean for the amount of artistic license allowed, see Keener, *Christobiography* (which also contains a useful discussion of some of the compositional and source-utilization techniques covered in this chapter), and (more briefly) Licona, *Why Are There Differences?* It's worth bearing in mind, however, that the Evangelists may not have been working to the same standards and expectations as the mainly elite authors Keener and Licona take as their examples.

It's also worth noting that while classifying the gospels as *bioi* has gained wide scholarly support, there are dissenting voices. Hooker, "Beginnings and Endings" qualifies the *bios* thesis by observing the extent to which the Gospels, unlike Graeco-Roman *bioi*, position themselves in relation to the narratives of the Hebrew Bible. Aune, *Literary Environment*, 22, 36–43 also notes the Jewish character of the Gospels and discusses possible biblical precedents for their kind of storytelling. Downing, *Doing Things with Words*, 118–32, 209–12, suggests that Mark borrowed popular storytelling techniques and that the Gospels would have had entertainment as a secondary objective (if only to keep their audiences' attention). Tolbert, *Sowing the Word*, goes considerably beyond this by arguing that Mark has most affinity with the ancient romance (or novel). This suggestion suffers from the fact that Mark's subject matter is remote from that of the typical ancient romance, but further points to the possibility that the Gospel authors may have combined elements from different genres even if the *bios* remains the primary one, which might in turn suggest that the Evangelists could have felt able to employ greater artistic license than elite biographers.

Scribal Copying

On textual variants in general, see Parker, *Living Text*. On their impact on the Synoptic Problem, see Head, "Textual Criticism" and Goodacre, *Synoptic Problem*, 99–102.

Consequences for Models of Synoptic Relationships

For a discussion of the possible impacts of oral tradition and memory on the composition of the gospels see Eve, *Behind the Gospels* and Eve, *Writing the Gospels*, 81–124.

Chapter 3 – The Two Document Hypothesis

Overview

For brief introductions to Two Document Hypothesis see Tuckett, "Current State," Tuckett, *Q and the History of Early Christianity*, 1–39; Kloppenborg,

Excavating Q, 11–54; Evans, "Two Source Hypothesis" and Goodacre, *Synoptic Problem*, 109–19. For a classic book-length treatment see Streeter, *Four Gospels*. For a critical account of the development of the Two Document Hypothesis (from an FH perspective), see Goulder, *Luke*, 28–37.

Markan Priority

On Markan Priority generally, see Goodacre, *Case Against Q*, 19–45 and/or *Synoptic Problem*, 56–83; Styler, "Priority of Mark"; Kloppenborg, *Excavating Q*, 11–54; Davies and Allison, *Saint Matthew*, 1:97–114; Eve, "Synoptic Problem Without Q?," 553–56; Evans, "Two Source Hypothesis," 28–35 and Streeter, *Four Gospels*, 157–69.

For the argument that Matthew and Luke improve on Mark, see Elder, *Media Matrix*, 61–93, 145–65 (concerning the oral residue in Mark which Matthew and Luke change in a more literary direction) and Damm, *Ancient Rhetoric*, esp. 59–60 but also the detailed rhetorical comparisons that follow.

For the argument from editorial fatigue, see Goodacre, "Fatigue in the Synoptics" and Styler, "Priority of Mark", 293–98, 304–9.

The Case for Q

1. The argument from order is perhaps most stridently stated by Streeter, *Four Gospels*, 183.

2. For the argument from alternating primitivity, see Streeter, *Four Gospels*, 183; Davies and Allison, *Saint Matthew*, 1:116; Kloppenborg, *Excavating Q*, 42–43; Tuckett, *Q and the History of Early Christianity*, 10, 13–14.

3. For the argument about the Infancy and Resurrection Narratives, see Kloppenborg, *Excavating Q*, 41.

4. For the argument about Matthean additions to Mark missing from Luke, see Kloppenborg, *Excavating Q*, 41; Tuckett, *Q and the History of Early Christianity*, 7–8; Evans, "Two Source Hypothesis," 44.

5. For the Unpicking Argument, see Downing, "Rehabilitation" and "Disagreements"; Tuckett, "Current State," 44–45 and Kirk, "Memory," 476.

But Is Q Necessary?

1. The Order Objection is dealt with more fully in chapter 5, but for some initial FH counterarguments see Farrer, "Dispensing," 74–85; Goodacre, *Synoptic Problem*, 123–31, Goulder, *Luke*, 38–41, and Matson, "Luke's Rewriting."

2. For FH counters to the argument from Alternating Primitivity, see Farrer, "Dispensing," 63–65; Goodacre, *Synoptic Problem*, 133–40 and *Case Against Q*, 133–51, and Watson, *Gospel Writing*, 160–63. On the specific example of the Lord's Prayer, see Olson, "Lord's Prayer." For a broader discussion of the methodological principles involves in determining who used whom, see Kloppenborg, "Conceptual Stakes," 22–29.

3. The Infancy Narratives are covered more fully in chapter 4, but for a brief treatment see Goodacre, *Synoptic Problem*, 132–33.

4. On Luke's alleged non-use of Matthean additions, see Goodacre, *Synoptic Problem*, 128–31 and Goulder, *Luke*, 43–45.

5. For the unpicking argument, see Olson, "Unpicking" and Goodacre, "Taking Our Leave." On the parable of the mustard seed, see Goulder, *Luke*, 41–43.

6. On the Distinctiveness of Q, see Goodacre, *Synoptic Problem*, 140–42 and Goulder, *Luke*, 50–51.

Chapter 3–Luke's Knowledge of Matthew

Beginnings

On Luke's use of Matthew and 1 Samuel (and other parts of the OT) in his infancy narratives see Goulder, *Luke*, 221–31, 246–49, 252–53, 255–61, 264–67. For Luke's use of Matthew's Annunciation Story, see also Watson,

Suggestions for Further Reading

Gospel Writing, 131–36. For the argument that Luke's Infancy Narrative is a mimetic transformation (i.e., imitation) of Matthew's, see McAdon, *Rhetorical Mimesis*, 120–60.

For Luke's use of Matthew in the John the Baptist material, baptism and temptation scenes, see Goodacre, *Synoptic Problem*, 151–53; Watson, *Gospel Writing*, 136–48; Goulder, *Luke*, 270–310; Kahl, "Gospel of Luke as Narratological Improvement."

Major and Minor Agreements

On the Major Agreements (aka Mark-Q overlaps), see Goodacre, *Synoptic Problem*, 148–51; Sanders and Davies, *Studying*, 78–82; Goodacre, "Taking Our Leave"; and Sanders, "Overlaps of Mark and Q." On the Beelzebul Controversy, see Eve, "Devil in the Detail."

On the Minor Agreements, see Goodacre, *Synoptic Problem*, 144–48; Sanders and Davies, *Studying*, 67–73; Goulder, *Luke* 47–50; Kahl, "Inclusive and Exclusive Agreements." On the striking agreement at Matt 26:67–68 see Goulder, *Luke*, 6–11 and "Two Significant Minor Agreements"; Black, "One Really Striking Minor Agreement." For a survey of scholarship on the minor agreements from a broadly 2DH perspective, see Neirynk, *Minor Agreements*, 13–48. On the difficulty of counting minor agreements see Boring, "'Minor Agreements.'" For 2DH counterarguments concerning minor agreements see Tuckett, *Q and the History of Early Christianity*, 28 and Kirk, "Memory," 475–58 (but note that neither scholar provides a convincing alternative explanation for the minor agreements, that memory interference can work both ways, and that Kirk fails to consider several other factors that might cause the spread of minor agreements to be uneven, such as the varying degree of Matthew's alterations to Mark in different passages).

For the argument concerning the surprising extent of verbatim agreement in parts of the Double Tradition, see Goodacre, "Two Good to be Q." For a response to Goodacre's argument from the 2DH perspective, see Kloppenborg, "Farrer/Mark without Q Hypothesis: A Response," 241–43.

Chapter 5–An Orderly Account

Hidden Parallels

The argument concerning Hidden Parallels is mainly my own (developed in chapter 6 of *Relating the Gospels*, where I call then "indirect parallels"), but shares quite a bit in common with Goulder's approach (in *Luke: A New Paradigm*) for many of the parallels considered. Goulder, however, envisages Luke working backwards through Matthew for part of his Central Section, whereas I suggest he was working forwards. On Luke's creativity, see Goulder, *Luke*, 75–78, 123–28.

Luke's Treatment of the Sermon on the Mount

See Matson, "Luke's Rewriting"; Goodacre, *Case Against Q*, 96–110; Watson, *Gospel Writing*, 163–68.

Luke's Central Section

For Luke as restoring Mark's Way of the Lord theme, see Goodacre, "Re-Walking." For earlier attempts to account for Luke's Central Section from an FH perspective, see Franklin, *Luke* 328–52 and Drury, *Tradition*, 138–64. For more recent FH discussions, see Watson, *Gospel Writing*, 163–216 and Matson, "Luke's Rewriting," 50–62. For other discussions of Luke's Central Section, see Evans, "Central Section", Moessner, *Lord of the Banquet,* and Egelkraut, *Jesus' Mission to Jerusalem*. Note, however, that the suggestion that Luke's Central Section is a Christian Deuteronomy, suggested by Evans and followed by Drury, has not found wide acceptance. For a sympathetic critique of this suggestion, see Franklin, *Luke*, 335–36.

Bibliography

Aune, David. *The New Testament in its Literary Environment*. Cambridge: James Clarke, 1988.
Black, Steve D. "One Really Striking Minor Agreement TIS ESTIN HO PAISAS SE in Matthew 26:68 and Luke 22:64." *NovT* 52 (2010) 313–33.
Boring, M. Eugene. "The 'Minor Agreements' and Their Bearing on the Synoptic Problem." In *New Studies in the Synoptic Problem*, edited by Paul Foster at al., 227–51. BETL 139. Leuven: Leuven University Press, 2011.
Brodie, Thomas L. *The Birthing of the New Testament: The Intertextual Development of the New Testament Writings*. NTM 1. Sheffield: Sheffield Phoenix, 2004.
Burridge, Richard A. *What Are the Gospels? A Comparison with Graeco-Roman Biography*. SNTSMS 70. Cambridge: Cambridge University Press, 1995.
Davies, W. D., and Dale C. Allison. *A Critical and Exegetical Commentary on the Gospel According to Saint Matthew*. ICC. Edinburgh: T. & T. Clark, 1988.
Derrenbacker, Robert A. *Ancient Compositional Practices and the Synoptic Problem*. BETL 186. Leuven: Peeters-Leuven, 2005.
———. "The 'External and Psychological Conditions under which the Synoptic Gospels Were Written': Ancient Compositional Practices and the Synoptic Problem." In *New Studies in the Synoptic Problem*, edited by Paul Foster at al., 435–57. BETL 139. Leuven: Leuven University Press, 2011.
Downing, F. Gerald. "Disagreements of Each Evangelist with the Minor Close Agreements of the Other Two." *ETL* 80 (2004) 445–69.
———. *Doing Things with Words in the First Christian Century*. JSNTSup 200. Sheffield: Sheffield Academic, 2000.
———. "Redaction Criticism: Josephus' Antiquities and the Synoptic Problem I." *JSNT* 8 (1980) 46–65.
———. "Redaction Criticism: Josephus' Antiquities and the Synoptic Problem II." *JSNT* 9 (1980) 29–48.
———. "Towards the Rehabilitation of Q." *NTS* 11 (1964) 169–81.
Dunn, James D. G. "Altering the Default Setting: Re-envisaging the Early Transmission of the Jesus Tradition." *NTS* 49 (2003) 139–75.
Drury, John. *Tradition and Design in Luke's Gospel: A Study in Early Christian Historiography*. London: Darton, Longman and Todd, 1976.
Egelkraut, Helmuth K. *Jesus' Mission to Jerusalem: A Redaction Critical Study of the Travel Narrative in the Gospel of Luke, Lk 9:51—19:48*. Frankfurt: Peter Lang, 1976.

Bibliography

Elder, Nicholas A. *The Media Matrix of Early Jewish and Christian Narrative.* LNTS 612. London: Bloomsbury T. & T. Clark, 2019.
Evans, Craig A. "The Two Source Hypothesis." In *The Synoptic Problem: Four Views*, edited by Stanley E. Porter and Bryan R. Dyer, 27–45. Grand Rapids: Baker Academic, 2016.
Evans, C. F. "The Central Section of St. Luke's Gospel." In *Studies in the Gospels: Essays in Memory of R. H. Lightfoot*, edited by D. E. Nineham, 37–53. Oxford: Blackwell, 1955.
Eve, Eric. *Behind the Gospels: Understanding the Oral Tradition.* London: SPCK, 2013.
———. "The Devil in the Detail: Exorcising Q from the Beelzebul Controversy." In *Marcan Priority without Q: Explorations in the Farrer Hypothesis*, edited by John C. Poirier and Jeff Peterson, 16–43. LNTS 455. London: Bloomsbury T. & T. Clark, 2015.
———. *Relating the Gospels: Memory, Imitation and the Farrer Hypothesis.* LNTS 592. London: Bloomsbury T. & T. Clark, 2021.
———. "The Synoptic Problem Without Q?" In *New Studies in the Synoptic Problem*, edited by Paul Foster at al., 551–70. BETL 139. Leuven: Leuven University Press, 2011.
———. *Writing the Gospels: Composition and Memory.* London: SPCK, 2016.
Farmer, William R. *The Synoptic Problem: A Critical Analysis.* Macon, GA: Mercer University Press, 1976.
Farrer, A. M. "On Dispensing with Q." In *Studies in the Gospels: Essays in Memory of R. H. Lightfoot*, edited by D. E. Nineham, 55–88. Oxford: Blackwell, 1955.
Franklin, Eric. *Luke: Interpreter of Paul, Critic of Matthew.* JSNTS 92. Sheffield: JSOT, 1994.
Gamble, Harry Y. *Books and Readers in the Early Church: A History of Early Christian Texts.* New Haven, CT: Yale University Press, 1988.
Goodacre, Mark. *The Case Against Q: Studies in Markan Priority and the Synoptic Problem.* Harrisburg, PA: Trinity, 2002.
———. "Fatigue in the Synoptics." *NTS* 44 (1998) 45–58.
———. "Re-Walking the 'Way of the Lord': Luke's Use of Mark and His Reaction to Matthew." In *Luke's Literary Creativity*, edited by in Mogens Müller and Jesper Tang Nielsen, 26–43. LNTS 550. London: Bloomsbury T. & T. Clark, 2016.
———. *The Synoptic Problem: A Way Through the Maze.* London: T. & T. Clark, 2001.
———. "Taking Our Leave of Mark-Q Overlaps: Major Agreements and the Farrer Theory." In *Gospel Interpretation and the Q-Hypothesis*, edited by Mogens Müller and Heike Omerzu, 201–22. LNTS 573. London: Bloomsbury T. & T. Clark, 2018.
———. "Too Good to Be Q: High Verbatim Agreement in the Double Tradition." In *Marcan Priority without Q: Explorations in the Farrer Hypothesis*, edited by John C. Poirier and Jeff Peterson, 82–100. LNTS 455. London: Bloomsbury T. & T. Clark, 2015.
Goulder, M. D. *Luke: A New Paradigm.* JSNTSup 20. Sheffield: Sheffield Academic Press, 1989.
———. "Two Significant Minor Agreements (Mat. 4:13 Par.; Mat. 26:67–68 Par.)." *NovT* 45 (2003) 365–73.
Gregory, Andrew. "What is Literary Dependence?" In *New Studies in the Synoptic Problem*, edited by Paul Foster at al., 87–114. BETL 139. Leuven: Leuven University Press, 2011.
Head, Peter M. "Textual Criticism and the Synoptic Problem." In *New Studies in the Synoptic Problem*, edited by Paul Foster at al., 115–56. BETL 139. Leuven: Leuven University Press, 2011.

Bibliography

Hengel, Martin. *The Four Gospels and the One Gospel of Jesus Christ: An Investigation of the Collection and Origin of the Canonical Gospels.* Translated by John Bowden. London: SCM, 2000.

Hooker, Morna D. "Beginnings and Endings." In *The Written Gospel*, edited by Markus Bockmuehl and David A. Hagner, 184–202. Cambridge: Cambridge University Press, 2005.

Huggins, Ronald V. "Matthean Posteriority: A Preliminary Proposal." *NovT* 34 (1992) 1–22.

Kahl, Werner. "The Gospel of Luke as Narratological Improvement of Synoptic Pre-Texts: The Narrative Introduction to the Jesus Story (Mark 1.1–8 Parr.)." In *Gospel Interpretation and the Q-Hypothesis*, edited by Mogens Müller and Heike Omerzu, 223–44. LNTS 573. London: Bloomsbury T. & T. Clark, 2018.

———. "Inclusive and Exclusive Agreements—Towards a Neutral Comparison of the Synoptic Gospels, Or: Minor Agreements as Misleading Category." In *Luke's Literary Creativity*, edited by Mogens Müller and Jesper Tang Nielsen, 44–78. LNTS 550. London: Bloomsbury T. & T. Clark, 2016.

Keener, Craig S. *Christobiography: Memory, Historyf and the Reliability of the Gospels.* Grand Rapids: Eerdmans, 2019.

Kirk, Alan. "Memory, Scribal Media, and the Synoptic Problem." In *New Studies in the Synoptic Problem*, edited by Paul Foster at al., 459–82. BETL 139. Leuven: Leuven University Press, 2011.

———. *Q in Matthew: Ancient Media, Memory, and Early Scribal Transmission of the Jesus Tradition.* LNTS 564. London: Bloomsbury T. & T. Clark, 2016.

Kloppenborg, John S. "Conceptual Stakes in the Synoptic Problem." In *Gospel Interpretation and the Q-Hypothesis*, edited by Mogens Müller and Heike Omerzu, 13–42. LNTS 573. London: Bloomsbury T. & T. Clark, 2018.

———. *Excavating Q: The History and Setting of the Sayings Gospel.* Edinburgh: T. & T. Clark, 2000.

———. "The Farrer/Mark without Q Hypothesis: A Response." In *Marcan Priority without Q: Explorations in the Farrer Hypothesis*, edited by John C. Poirier and Jeff Peterson, 226–44. LNTS 455. London: Bloomsbury T. & T. Clark, 2015.

———. "Variation and Reproduction of the Double Tradition and an Oral Q?" *ETL* 83 (2007) 53–80.

Knauer, Georg Nicolaus. "Vergil's *Aeneid* and Homer." *GRBS* 5 (1964) 61–84.

Licona, Michael R. *Why Are There Differences in the Gospels? What We Can Learn from Ancient Biography.* New York: Oxford University Press, 2017.

MacEwen, Robert K. *Matthean Posteriority: An Exploration of Matthew's Use of Mark and Luke as a Solution to the Synoptic Problem.* LNTS 501. London: Bloomsbury T. & T. Clark, 2015.

MacDonald, Dennis R. *The Gospels and Homer: Imitation of Greek Epic in Mark and Luke-Acts.* NTGL 1. Lanham, MD: Rowman & Littlefield, 2015.

———. "The Shipwrecks of Odysseus and Paul." *NTS* 45 (1999) 88–107.

MacDonald, Dennis R., ed. *Mimesis and Intertextuality in Antiquity and Christianity.* SAC. Harrisburg, PA: Trinity, 2001.

Matson, Mark A. "Luke's Rewriting of the Sermon on the Mount." In *Questioning Q*, edited by Mark S. Goodacre and Nicholas Perrin, 43–70. London: SPCK, 2004.

Bibliography

McAdon, Brad. *Rhetorical Mimesis and the Mitigation of Early Christian Conflicts: Examining the Influence that Greco-Roman Mimesis May Have in the Composition of Matthew, Luke, and Acts*. Eugene, OR: Pickwick, 2018.

Moessner, David P. *Lord of the Banquet: The Literary and Theological Significance of the Lukan Travel Narrative*. Minneapolis: Augsburg Fortress, 1989.

Neirynck, Frans. *The Minor Agreements of Matthew and Luke against Mark with A Cumulative List*. BETL 37. Leuven: Leuven University Press, 1974.

O'Leary, Anne M. *Matthew's Judaization of Mark Examined in the Context of the Use of Sources in Greco-Roman Antiquity*. LNTS 323. London: T. & T. Clark, 2006.

Olson, Ken. "Luke 11.2–4: The Lord's Prayer (Abridged Version)." In *Marcan Priority without Q: Explorations in the Farrer Hypothesis*, edited by John C. Poirier and Jeff Peterson, 101–18. LNTS 455. London: Bloomsbury T. & T. Clark, 2015.

———. "Unpicking on the Farrer Theory." In *Questioning Q*, edited by Mark Goodacre and Nicholas Perrin, 127–50. London: SPCK, 2004.

Parker, David C. *The Living Text of the Gospels*. Cambridge: Cambridge University Press, 1997.

Pelling, C. B. R. "Plutarch's Adaptation of His Source-Material." *JHS* 100 (1980) 127–40.

——— "Plutarch's Method of Work in the Roman Lives." *JHS* 99 (1979) 74–96.

Porter, Stanley E., and Bryan R. Dyer, eds. *The Synoptic Problem: Four Views*. Grand Rapids: Baker Academic, 2016.

Russell, D. A. "De Imitatione." In *Creative Imitation and Latin Literature*, edited by David West and Tony Woodman, 1–16. Cambridge: Cambridge University Press, 1979.

Sanders, E. P. "The Overlaps of Mark and Q and the Synoptic Problem." *NTS* 19 (1972) 453–65.

Sanders, E. P., and Margaret Davies. *Studying the Synoptic Gospels*. London: SCM, 1989.

Streeter, Burnett Hillman. *The Four Gospels: A Study of Origins Treating of the Manuscript Tradition, Sources, Authorship, and Dates*. London: Macmillan, 1926.

Styler, G. M. "Excursus IV: The Priority of Mark." In *The Birth of the New Testament* by C. F. D. Moule, 285–316. 3rd ed. London: A&C Black, 1981.

Tolbert, Mary Ann. *Sowing the Gospel: Mark's World in Literary-Historical Perspective*. Minneapolis: Fortress, 1989.

Tuckett, Christopher M. "The Current State of the Synoptic Problem." In *New Studies in the Synoptic Problem*, edited by Paul Foster at al., 9–50. BETL 139. Leuven: Leuven University Press, 2011.

———. *Q and the History of Early Christianity*. Edinburgh: T. & T. Clark, 1997.

———. *The Revival of the Griesbach Hypothesis: An Analysis and Appraisal*. SNTSMS 44; Cambridge: Cambridge University Press, 1983.

Watson, Francis. *Gospel Writing: A Canonical Perspective*. Grand Rapids: Eerdmans, 2013.

Winn, Adam. *Mark and the Elijah-Elisha Narrative: Considering the Practice of Greco-Roman Imitation in the Search for Markan Source Material*. Eugene, OR: Pickwick, 2010.

Winsbury, Rex. *The Roman Book: Books, Publishing and Performance in Classical Rome*. London: Bristol Classical, 2009.

www.ingramcontent.com/pod-product-compliance
Lightning Source LLC
Chambersburg PA
CBHW020856160426
43192CB00007B/947